W9-BGE-354

To Declare
God's Forgiveness

To Declare God's Forgiveness

Toward a Pastoral Theology of Reconciliation

Clark Hyde

Morehouse Barlow
Wilton

The author expressly thanks the following for their permissions:

Academic Press
 An Introduction to Theories of Personality by Robert B. Ewen.
 Copyright © 1980
Harcourt, Brace, Jovanovich
 from "Little Gidding" in *Four Quarters, Copyright* © 1943 by T.S.
 Eliot; renewed 1971 by Esme Valerie Eliot. Reprinted by permission of
 Harcourt, Brace, Jovanovich, Inc.
Harper and Row
 Soul Friend by Kenneth Leech. Copyright © 1977; *Stages of Faith* by
 James W. Fowler. Copyright © 1981
Harvard University Press
 In a Different Voice by Carol Gilligan. Copyright © 1982
Liturgical Conference
 The Rite of Penance: Commentaries, Vol. I, II, III, Copyright © 1975.
 The Liturgical Conference, 806 Rhode Island Avenue, Washington
 D.C. 20018. All rights reserved.
Michael Glazier, Inc.
 Sign of Reconciliation and Conversion, by Monika Hellwig. Copyright
 © 1982
National Council of Churches
 From the Revised Standard Version of the Bible. Copyrighted 1946,
 1952 © 1971, 1973
Society for Research in Child Development
 A Longitudinal Study of Moral Judgment by Ann Colby. Monographs
 of S.R.C.D. Serial No. 200, Vol. 46, Nos. 1-2
W.H. Freeman and Company
 Roots of Caring, Sharing, and Helping by Paul Mussen and Nancy
 Eisenberg-Berg. Copyright © 1977

Copyright © 1984 Clark Hyde

All rights reserved. No part of this publication may be reproduced, stored in a
retrieval system, or transmitted in any form or by any means, electronic,
mechanical, photocopying, recording, or otherwise, without the prior permission of the copyright owner.

Morehouse Barlow Co., Inc.
78 Danbury Road
Wilton, Connecticut 06897

ISBN 0-8192-1348-9

Library of Congress Catalog Card Number 84-60626

Composition by The Publishing Nexus Incorporated, 1200 Boston Post
Road, Guilford, Connecticut 06437
Printed in the United States of America

To the People of
St. Peter's Parish, Delaware, Ohio

Contents

Foreword

ANGLICANISM did not, like some communions, reject the practice of private confession to a priest at the time of the Reformation. The Book of Common Prayer 1979, however, gives a more prominent place to the rite and provides more ample directions and more explicit teaching concerning the rite than any previous Prayer Book.

Various early Anglican Reformation formularies, such as the Ten Articles set forth in 1536, the Bishops' Book of 1537, the King's Book of 1543, and "Cranmer's Catechism" of 1548, included teaching about Penance, setting forth Penance along with the sacraments of Baptism and Eucharist as a sacrament necessary to salvation.

The 1548 Order of the Communion dealt with the practice of private confession in one of its exhortations. It is not called a sacrament, nor is it set forth as necessary to salvation. Instead it is commended to those who cannot quiet their consciences by "their humble confession to God, and the general confession to the church":

> And if there be any of you whose conscience is troubled and grieved in anything, lacking comfort or counsel, let him come to me, or to some other discreet and learned priest taught in the law of God, and confess and open his sin and grief secretly, that he may receive such ghostly counsel, advice, and comfort that his conscience may be relieved, and that of us, as of the ministers of God and of the church, he may receive comfort and absolution, to the satisfaction

of his mind and avoiding of all scruple and doubtfulness: requiring such as shall be satisfied with a general confession not to be offended with them that do use to their further satisfying the auricular and secret confession to the priest; nor those also which think needful or convenient, for the quietness of their own consciences, particularly to open their sins to the priest, to be offended with them that are satisfied with their humble confession to God, and the general confession to the church: but in all things to follow and keep the rule of charity, and every man to be satisfied with his own conscience, not judging other men's minds or acts whereas he hath no warrant of God's Word for the same.

The catechism of the 1549 Book of Common Prayer listed Baptism and the Eucharist only as the sacraments necessary to salvation and made no mention of Penance. This first Prayer Book, however, made provision for the continuation of the practice of private confession. It retained a slightly modified form of the exhortation in the Order of the Communion commending the practice to those with troubled consciences, and included in the Order for the Visitation of the Sick a rubric, "Here shall the sick person make a special confession, if he feel his conscience troubled with any weighty matter." Included in that rite is a form of absolution with the direction, "the same form of absolution shall be used in all private confessions." This declaratory form was based partly on a form in the Sarum rite for the visitation of the sick and partly on the absolution in the Consultation, the German Church Order set forth by Hermann von Wied, the reforming archbishop of Cologne:

> Our Lord Jesus Christ, who hath left power to his Church to absolve all sinners, which truly repent and believe in him: of his great mercy forgive thee thine offences; and by his authority committed to me, I absolve thee from all thy sins, in the Name of the Father, and of the Son, and of the Holy Ghost. Amen.

The 1549 Prayer Book did not contain ordination rites. The preface to the rites published in 1550 stated that the essential matter of ordination is "public prayer, with imposition of hands." In the rite for the ordination of a priest, however, the laying on of hands is accompanied not by prayer but by a form the beginning of which was associated with a peculiar second laying on of hands after the Communion which had entered the rite in the thirteenth century: "Receive the Holy Ghost: whose sins thou dost forgive, they are forgiven, and whose sins thou dost retain, they are retained."

Evidently from the first the provisions of the Prayer Book in relation to private confession were controversial, and they were tempered somewhat in the 1552 revision. The exhortation was altered to read:

> And because it is requisite that no man should come to the Holy Communion but with a full trust in God's mercy, and with a quiet conscience, therefore if there be any of you which by the means aforesaid cannot quiet his own conscience, but requireth further comfort or counsel; then let him come to me, or some other discreet and learned minister of God's word and open his grief that he may receive such ghostly counsel, advice, and comfort as his conscience may be relieved and that by the ministry of God's Word he may receive comfort and the benefit of absolution, to the quieting of his conscience, and avoiding of all scruple and doubtfulness.

The rubric directing a sick person to make a special confession if troubled in conscience was retained, but the sentence preceding the absolution was revised to read "After which confession the priest shall absolve him after this sort [1549: after this form]." Mention of use of this absolution in other private confessions was deleted.

Puritans objected to the term "absolution," and particularly to the form "I absolve thee" in the absolution of the Order for the Visitation of the Sick. The 1662 Prayer Book added a qualification to the rubric preceding the form, "After which Confession, the Priest shall absolve him (if he humbly and heartily desire it) after this sort."

Since the Prayer Book provided no form for use in private confession other than the absolution, some clergy compiled their own rites. Opposition to private confession, to the words "priest" and "absolution," and particularly to the form of absolution in the Order for the Visitation of the Sick began to spread beyond the bounds of the Puritan party. Use of these words and/or provision for a special confession were omitted from an overwhelming majority of the Prayer Book revisions and proposals for revision of the eighteenth century. Provisions were omitted altogether from the liturgy of the Nonjuror Thomas Deacon and the liturgical archaeologist William Whiston as well as from Latitudinarian proposals and John Wesley's *The Sunday Service of the Methodists in North America*. Regardless of churchmanship eighteenth-century Anglicans were generally uncomfortable with the words "priest" and "absolution," and few availed themselves of the opportunity to make a special confession.

In the first American Book of Common Prayer, that of 1789, the conclusion of the exhortation was revised to read, "let him come to me, or to some other minister of God's word, and open his grief; that he may receive such godly counsel and advice, as may tend to the quieting of his conscience, and the removing of all scruple and doubtfulness." The rubric concerning a special confession and the form of absolution were removed from the visitation rite. The idea of a special confession followed by absolution was not deleted altogether from the book, however. A rite for the visitation of prisoners from the Prayer Book of the Church of Ireland was incorporated, in which the "minister" is instructed to move the prisoner to make a confession, and "After his confession, the minister shall declare to him the pardoning mercy of God, in the form which is used in the Communion-service." The 1792 revision of the rite for the ordination of priests provided an alternative form for use at the laying on of hands which contained no reference to the power to forgive sins.

The resurgence of the practice of private confession in Anglicanism was largely a result of the Oxford Movement. Despite some vehement opposition the practice of private confession was defended and encouraged, and an increasing number of people accepted the practice of regular self-examination and confession as a component in a rule of life.

The 1928 American Prayer Book revision dropped the form for the visitation of prisoners, but included a rubric modeled on that of the English book in the Order for the Visitation of the Sick, "Then shall the sick person be moved to make a special confession of his sins, if he feel his conscience troubled with any matter; after which confession, on evidence of his repentance, the Minister shall assure him of God's mercy and forgiveness."

Other Prayer Book revisions of the period expanded the

section on confession in the Order for the Visitation of the Sick. The 1928 English book provided a form for the confession of the penitent which was a radically condensed version of the Roman Catholic Counter-Reformation form. This was picked up in the Scottish revision of 1929. The Canadian 1959 book and the Australian 1978 book also provided similar forms for the use of the penitent in the context of the Order for the Visitation of the Sick.

The 1954 South African book was the first Book of Common Prayer to separate the provision for confession from the Order for the Visitation of the Sick and to give it a separate heading, "A Form of Confession and Absolution." The rite was introduced by a rubric concerning the secrecy of the confessional, another stating that the church does not for forgiveness require confession before a priest, and a third which is a condensed version of the section on private confession from the 1548–1549 exhortation. The texts consist of an initial blessing by the priest and a form of confession for the penitent, revised from the sixteenth-century Roman rite, followed by the absolution printed in the Order for the Visitation of the Sick in previous Books of Common Prayer. Before the absolution the priest is to give "such counsel and penance as may be convenient," and after it to dismiss the penitent with a blessing. This rite, somewhat revised, was picked up in the 1960 Book of Common Prayer for the Church of India, Pakistan, Burma and Ceylon.

The 1979 American Book of Common Prayer provides more explicit teaching and more adequate provisions for confession than earlier books. The relevant section in the exhortation has been revised. Having urged self-examination in preparation for Communion, the exhortation proceeds,

> And if, in your preparation, you need help and counsel, then go and open your grief to a discreet and understanding priest, and confess your sins, that you may receive the benefit of absolution, and spiritual counsel and advice; to the removal of scruple and doubt, the assurance of pardon, and the strengthening of your faith.

The Catechism of the 1979 book lists "reconciliation of a penitent" among the "other sacramental rites [which] evolved in the Church under the guidance of the Holy Spirit." The Catechism also contains a question and answer related to this sacramental rite:

Q. What is Reconciliation of a Penitent?
A. Reconciliation of a Penitent, or Penance, is the rite in which those who repent of their sins may confess them to God in the presence of a priest, and receive the assurance of pardon and the grace of absolution.

Two forms are provided for the rite. They are not hidden in an Order for the Visitation of the Sick but listed aong the Pastoral Offices under a separate heading, "The Reconciliation of a Penitent." The title puts the emphasis on "reconciliation" rather than on "confession" or "penance." The Catechism, the exhortation, and the section "Concerning the Rite" which is printed just before it suggest that it is available for all who repent, not just for the sick or for those who cannot satisfy their own consciences. Though not necessary in the same way as Baptism and the Eucharist, the Reconciliation of a Penitent is a means of grace available for all who desire it.

Clark Hyde has done a great service for the Church in providing this excellent introduction and commentary on the new rite. He places the rite in an ecumenical context and brings to bear learnings from the growing body of literature in spiritual direction, adult developmental psychology, and faith development. He gives helpful suggestions as to how this sacramental rite may best be used and how priests and penitents can best prepare for it. This book should be required reading for all seminary students and parish priests, and it will be helpful to many others seeking to grow spiritually and desiring to make better use of this means of grace.

Marion J. Hatchett

Preface

THIS work represents an important point on my own journey as a Christian and as a priest, and it seems appropriate for me to pause a moment to look back at the route I have travelled. Having become an Episcopalian while an undergraduate, in a kind of conversion experience, I began to feel the pull of something I now identify as a vocation to the ordained ministry. I am grateful to those who discerned and nurtured that call and helped me struggle with it. Finding myself in seminary, in the Graduate Theological Union in Berkeley, California, I came under the influence of a number of superb pastors and teachers. Outstanding among them, at least insofar as this work is concerned, was Massey Hamilton Shepherd, Jr., a scholar of immense gifts and remarkable influence. Dr. Shepherd opened to me, as to a whole generation of students, the riches of our liturgical tradition and an appreciation for the theology on which it is founded. We are all in his debt, and I gladly acknowledge my small share of that debt.

Following ordination and my first cure, I began to discern a need for a deeper understanding of what I was about as a priest. Providentially, I discovered the discipline of pastoral theology and began mining its riches. Among those whose work in that field gave me the most help was that of Urban T. Holmes III. In 1979 I met Terry, as he wished to be known by friends and students, and was delighted to find him a willing and gracious mentor. With his support, I entered the S.T.M. program at the School of Theology of the University of the South, planning a degree in pastoral theology, with Terry to serve as my advisor. With many others in the Episcopal Church and beyond, I felt a great loss at Dean Holmes's untimely death in 1981.

The faculty at Sewanee has been as helpful as I could wish in enabling me to complete this work, which is substantially the thesis for the S.T.M. Craig Anderson served ably as my advisor, helping me choose a topic and pare it down to a manageable size, making very helpful comments on the draft. I also am most grateful to Marion Hatchett, dean of Epicopal liturgiologists, who served as second reader, commentator, and writer of the Foreword. Professor Walter Bouman, of Trinity Lutheran Seminary, Columbus, Ohio, read the material on the Lutheran Book of Worship, and his help is very much appreciated. I also want to pay tribute to Professor Don Armentrout, director of the Sewanee graduate program, for his friendship, support, and encouragement. Needless to say (though in a Preface like this, one always does), any errors are entirely of my own begetting.

The thesis was written in October and November of 1983, during a sabbatical leave granted me by the Vestry of St. Peter's Parish, Delaware, Ohio, which I have the honor to serve as Rector. The Right Reverend William Black, Bishop of Southern Ohio, generously provided a grant to assist the project, in addition to grants I have received over the years from the Continuing Education Grants Committee of my diocese. The support of my bishop and colleagues has meant much to me, and I thank them. Chaplain James Leslie of Ohio Wesleyan University provided an invaluable service—a quiet place to read and write. My wife, Janet, gave me not only the sort of encouragement one counts on from one's spouse, but a great deal of technical expertise gleaned from her experience writing college psychology texts. My children, Margaret and Luke, were very patient with their father during the time of writing, and they have made a real contribution as well.

The writing of this work has also reminded me of the many wise and faithful priests whom I have been blessed in consulting as confessors or spiritual directors over the years. I am sure that their examples have formed and molded me in ways I am not fully aware. Likewise, I know that I have gained much in a decade in the ministry through various fine colleagues, Episcopal and ecumenical. The art of ministry is not so much taught as it is absorbed by one's relationships with significant models and mentors. I rejoice in the fruitful professional relationships I have known.

In many ways the greatest contribution to this work has been made by the people of St. Peter's Church. I have come to believe that pastoral theology, of all disciplines, cannot and ought not be done in a vacuum. My pastoral experience is an integral part of my work, and without all those who have shared their lives and their faith with me this book could not have been written. It is a joy to serve as their priest and, over the years, they have given me far more than I can have given them. I bless the name of the Lord for the people of St. Peter's Church and to them this work is affectionately dedicated.

Clark Hyde
Holy Week 1984

I

Introduction

AMONG the many new things in the Episcopal Church's *Book of Common Prayer* (1979) (which as often as not were actually old things revived) are two orders for "The Reconciliation of a Penitent." Although the possibility for private or auricular confession had been present, in theory, since the English Reformation, this is one of the first times a province of the Anglican Communion has actually set forth an order for the rite in its official liturgy. Given the significance of this step, it is disappointing that little in the way of commentary or interpretative material appeared with the order.

Indeed, there has been little written on the whole subject of confession and reconciliation by Anglicans in the last twenty years. Episcopal priests desiring to become more informed about the rite of Reconciliation, in order to prepare their parishioners for it, would find little guidance within their own tradition. There is a 1974 book by Kenneth Ross, late Vicar of All Saints Church, Margaret Street, London, entitled *Hearing Confessions*, but it is not widely available in this country. The only other work generally available is the Appendix in Kenneth Leech's *Soul Friend*, a treatise on spiritual direction. It is the purpose of the present work to fill the gap and provide the contemporary Episcopal priest a theological rationale for the rite of Reconciliation, with suggestions how people can be prepared for it and how it may be administered.

In doing this, I hope to produce a theological work that clearly stands within what Martin Thornton calls the English

1

(Anglican) pastoral tradition. Accordingly, I make certain assumptions that ought to be clearly stated at the outset. First, I assume that there *is* something we can call the Anglican tradition, sufficiently coherent to provide guidance for ministry. I believe our heritage as Anglicans provides a rich variety of resources for pastoral practice and for the development of what the late Urban T. Holmes III might have called a "pastoral sensibility" out of which we can work. Further, I assume that the pastoral task, that is, the work of those engaged in ministry, is, among other things, to prepare Christians for the sacraments and to administer them. This ministry is primarily, but by no means exclusively, exercised by the ordained. In the present instance, while it is clear from tradition and the rubrics that a priest is the normative minister of Reconciliation, it is nonetheless possible, and perhaps desirable, that laypersons be involved in preparing people for it. Certainly, all the People of God together make up the community within which sacramental reconciliation is a manifestation of God's grace and presence.

Finally, I assume that in pastoral ministry we are informed and guided by the classical "Anglican tripod" as modified into a quadrilateral by John Wesley, namely, Scripture, tradition, reason, and experience. We begin with the Scriptures, seen both through the best modern critical scholarship available, and through the Church's tradition, that two-thousand-year story of the efforts of God's people to understand and live out the Good News contained in it. Reason means, for the twentieth-century Christian, using the best resources provided by the culture, especially those that help us better understand the human creation. The work of natural and social scientists, though not determinative of our theological convictions, is a continuing source of information, concepts, resources, and challenges. Finally, no Christian theology worthy of the name can ignore the actual experience of Christians at prayer, at work, at witness in the world, for it is so often in this experience that the power of the Holy Spirit, given to us in Baptism, is made manifest.

The methods I propose to use in this study include historical survey, reflection on the tradition, exegesis of the liturgical texts, research into related disciplines, and application to the concrete pastoral situation. I believe this methodology to be consistent with the renewed and developing discipline of pastoral theology, whose prime Anglican exemplar was Urban T. Holmes III.

In our historical survey, my prime concern is to understand how we, in this branch of the Church, found our way to the present situation. I want to focus on the theological issues, concentrating not, for example, on the texts by which sacramental reconciliation was administered, but on the theological rationale behind them. What was it that our ancestors in the faith believed they were doing? How can their understanding illuminate ours? The foundation of this reflection on the tradition is, of course, scriptural. Again and again, we will be referred back to the Gospel proclamation both of our need for repentance and of God's loving mercy in reconciling us to himself in Jesus Christ.

In our exegesis of the liturgical texts, this concern for theology will continue. We are not so much interested in sources and historical evolution as in their meaning. What is the "implicit theology" of the Prayer Book rite for the Reconciliation of a Penitent? It is my conviction that we will be enriched if we study the other rites of Reconciliation that our sister communions have developed, or about which they have reflected. In particular, we will pay serious attention to the constitution and rationale of the Roman Catholic *Rite of Penance* and the order for Individual Confession and Forgiveness in *The Lutheran Book of Worship*.

Acting on the hypothesis that, in our age, sacramental reconciliation is most likely to be used by persons seeking to grow in their faithfulness as Christians, we will examine two disciplines that speak of growth and personal maturation. From within the Church, I will survey the literature of spiritual direction and ascetical theology. Within the culture, there is a growing literature of adult developmental psychology that might be useful to us. I will look specifically at the contributions of the psychoanalytic tradition (exemplified by Freud, Jung, and Erikson), the cognitive-developmental approach (Piaget) and its issue in theories of moral development (Kohlberg and his critics), and a body of research generally known as social learning theory. Closer to home, as it were, is the work now being done on faith development, notably by James Fowler, in an effort to bring together quite explicitly the findings of the social sciences and the religious community's experience of faith. I will attempt to synthesize these various theories into a model of Christian growth that can inform pastoral practice.

I will attempt to draw all this research together to inform the Church's ministry of sacramental reconciliation. To do this, we must examine the pastoral context of Reconciliation, which involves the nature of the pastoral task, the role of the community, and the ministry of the priest as confessor. I then want to suggest ways in which our model of Christian development can be applied to this ministry. Finally, I will suggest some practical considerations for the preparation of people for Reconciliation and the administration of the rite itself.

A short note on titles may be in order. The rite, or sacrament, in question has gone by at least three titles historically: Confession, Penance, and Reconciliation. Like the many titles of the Holy Eucharist, these actually refer to the three actions that have been understood traditionally to make up the rite from the earliest times. Confession refers, of course, to the actual confession of sins by one who is repentant and desires to be restored to full communion with the Church and with God. Penance refers to the satisfaction, the action that manifests the penitent's sincere desire to be restored, usually an action proposed by the minister of the rite. Reconciliation technically refers to the absolution, to the restoration of the now-forgiven penitent to full communion with the Body of Christ. In this work, we will use the term Reconciliation most frequently, but will refer to the rite by its other titles when the context demands it.

Another problem of language needs to be addressed, as well. For most of Christian history, the language of theology has been thoroughly sexist, meaning that the male is understood linguistically to be the normative human being. The language used about the ordained ministry has been, as it were, appropriately sexist, as all deacons, presbyters, and bishops were male. This is no longer the case in the Episcopal Church. Therefore, I shall be using gender-inclusive language for all references to Christians and the clergy. I shall make no effort, however, to "clean up" the language of those I quote; they will be allowed to speak in their own voices and with their own words.

Before we begin, then, let me restate the problem I wish to address and my thesis in addressing it. The problem is the absence of guidance to priests of the Episcopal Church, and other persons involved, as to the appropriate preparation for and administration of the Reconciliation of a Penitent in the 1979 *Book of Common Prayer*. That rite has a rationale and a history that, together, define our present situation. This situation will be illuminated, I believe, by a consideration of the rite in other churches that practice it.

My thesis is that we can start from the present situation, once we understand it, and enrich our pastoral understanding of the rite by drawing together insights from spiritual direction and theories of human development, especially those that concentrate on moral and faith development. I want to test my assumption that the pastoral use of the sacrament should be related to the developmental stage of the persons involved. Having correlated these various approaches and resources, I hope to produce a working pastoral theology of Reconciliation in the Episcopal Church for the information and use of those who exercise this significant Christian ministry. That ministry is expressed in the bishop's charge at the ordination of a priest, "to declare God's forgiveness to penitent sinners." The proclamation of that forgiveness, in word, deed, and sacramental action, is, I believe, essential to the nature of the whole Christian Church, which is called to be an instrument of God's loving reconciliation of the whole world in Christ.

II

Reconciliation in History

IN this section, we will survey the historical development of the rite of Reconciliation from the Apostolic Age to the present, using the helpful scheme provided in Poschmann's classic work.[1] In the period of Christian Antiquity, roughly the first through the sixth centuries A.D., we see spread of the Gospel, the development of doctrines of forgiveness of sin, a concern for ecclesiastical discipline, and the development of canonical public penance as a means of dealing with post-baptismal sin. In the early Middle Ages, there was a shift away from the older forms to private penance, especially through the widespread influence of the Celtic Penitentials. During the Scholastic Period, or the High Middle Ages, the rite of Penance as it had evolved was given a theoretical and doctrinal foundation, which was quite solid by the time of the Reformation. While Poschmann goes on to elaborate a fourth period in Catholic penitential practice, Trent to the present, we will diverge and follow the trail of the Reformation, especially in its English form. Our study of Anglicanism will bring us to the present, which might well be regarded as a fifth period, not only for Roman Catholicism, but for all Western Christianity, namely, the period after Vatican II.

Christian Antiquity

Throughout the history of Israel, it was proclaimed repeatedly that God in his holiness and love forgives the sins of his

6

people. No more eloquent testimony to this conviction can be
found than Psalm 103:

> He does not deal with us according to our sins,
>   nor requite us according to our iniquities.
> For as the heavens are high above the earth,
>   so great is his steadfast love
>   to those who fear him;
> as far as the east is from the west,
>   so far does he remove our transgressions from us.

For most of the Hebrew Scriptures, however, this hope remains in
the future. Forgiveness of sins in this life remains a hope to be
achieved in the coming messianic age.

Jesus comes into human history proclaiming that the age to
come is even now breaking in upon humanity, and with it the
forgiveness of sin. His primary proclamation is, "The time is
fulfilled, and the kingdom of God is at hand; repent and believe in
the gospel" (Mark 1:15). This becomes the keynote of the preaching of Jesus and of the faith of those who received it.

> The Gospel of the kingdom which Chirst summoned men to
> believe in is the good news that God, in his forgiving love, is among
> men, healing them of the sickness of their sin by the power that is
> solely his. Jesus is the bringer of forgiveness.[2]

The breaking in of the kingdom demanded a radical decision, and the early Christian community required that it be made
in "faith accompanied by moral conversion."[3] This choice was
made by the believer in baptism, in which the faithful were incorporated into the eschatological community, the Body of Christ, in
which they became one with him and shared in his victory over sin
and death. Thus, from the beginning, we see in the New Testament an emphasis on the eschatological and corporate aspects of
the forgiveness of sins, although we cannot say that there is one
specific biblical doctrine of reconciliation. There is, rather, the
experience of reconciliation with God in Christ, described in a
variety of ways.

We see also from the beginning a tension between the
rigorous demands of the kingdom and the recognition that the
Church must exist in the world, a world dominated by the fact of
sin. The Christian ministry of reconciliation will take place among

the very sinners whom Christ came to call to righteousness. To the Church Jesus commits the "power of the keys," the power of binding and loosing sins (Matthew 16:18, 18:18). In the Johannine tradition, this power and authority is a sign of the Holy Spirit's presence in the Church (John 20:19–23). Thus, forgiveness is not just a matter between the individual believer and God, but is effected by the mediation of the Church. Yet this Church, constituted by Baptism, is full of sinners. In the first flush of the expectation of an imminent *parousia*, Christians seem to have believed that after baptism a sinless life was possible, but the Christian community came very quickly to a modification of this view. The result was concern for ecclesiastical discipline. As Telfer puts it,

> by the end of the first Christian century, many had come to recognize that the Christian life, while it must ever cling to the pursuit of sinlessness, needed still, and that on account of post-baptismal sins, to be a penitent life.[4]

We can see this concern for discipline most clearly, among early writers, in St. Paul's Corinthian correspondence. In 1 Corinthians 5:1–8, a notorious sinner is to be excluded from the community: "You are to deliver this man to Satan for the destruction of the flesh, that his spirit may be saved in the day of the Lord Jesus" (5:5). This "excommunication" is not for judgment, however, but to induce repentance; the hope of reincorporation into the community is held out. In 2 Corinthians 2, we read of just such a restoration. Whether or not the reference is to the same man, it is clear that adequate repentance brings forgiveness and a restoration to the communion *koinonia* of the Church. Paul is quite clear that ecclesiastical forgiveness is possible, although we cannot say how that is related in Paul's mind to the ultimate forgiveness of God.[5]

On the other hand, there is some suggestion in the New Testament that it is possible to sin so gravely that one is put altogether beyond the mercy of God and the communion of his Church. Often cited as examples are the statements about the unforgivable sin "against the Holy Spirit" (Matthew 12:31f and parallels), and the statement in Hebrews that "it is impossible to restore again to repentance those who have once been enlightened...if they then commit apostasy" (Hebrews 6:4–6). However, it is consistent with the rest of the New Testament and with the practice of the early Chuch to recognize that the only sin that is literally unforgivable is a willful impenitence that seeks no forgiveness. Otherwise, it seems that God always holds out to the repentant the promise of restoration and renewal, and that the Church is called to exercise this ministry of reconciliation.

Nevertheless, the "rigorist" tendency in the Christian Church is here from the beginning and is to be found to the present day. This point of view, in matters of Church discipline, opposes making reconciliation after post-baptismal sin too easy, both to avoid compromising the Church's high moral standards and to prevent mercy on the erring from inciting other Christians to sin. Opposed to this view is the "liberal" or "lenient" view, which wants always to hold out hope to those who fall. The Church began wrestling with this tension in the first century, and has so wrestled ever since.[6]

The tension was resolved by the gradual development of disciplinary procedures. The probable source of these procedures was, as is so often the case, the Synagogue. In first-century Judaism, the community dealt with violations of its standards by expulsion, corporal punishment, or even stoning to death. These procedures were modified by the Christian Church, but it was still clearly the *community* that administered them. The form of discipline varied from place to place, but common penitential exercises were prayer, fasting, almsgiving, and the public confession of sin. Penitents who had been expelled from the fellowship were re-admitted when the congregation believed them to have shown adequate repentance. Evidence for such discipline can be found not only in the Corinthian references, but also in Acts 5, 2 Thessalonians 3:14–15, Titus 3:11–12, and various places in Revelation. In Matthew's Gospel, disciplinary material is collected in Chapter 18. It is also clear from Scripture that the emerging "official ministers," bishops and presbyters, were increasingly charged with judgment in matters of discipline on behalf of the community.[7]

This system, which had developed in a pragmatic fashion, was given its first theoretical formulation in the second century and became a matter of debate among those holding more and less rigorous views. This period was characterized by certain themes. First, there were very high standards for baptism, as seen in the evolution of a long and rigorous catechumenate. Second, there was the working out of a doctrine of Second Repentance for grave post-baptismal sins, as seen, for example, in the *Shepherd of Hermas*. Such a repentance acquired the technical name *exomologesis*, that is, "confession," and was the Church's pastoral response to the problems of grave post-baptismal sin. It was supported by a revision of the prevailing eschatology, in which the Church was seen as a mixed body of saints and sinners that God would perfect as a preconditiion to the Lord's return. Finally, distinctions were developed between lesser sins that were forgiven through continuous ordinary repentance and grave sins that could only be forgiven by *exomologesis*. According to Telfer, this development had two corollaries:

> The first is that however difficult it may be to set the boundary between the two categories of sins, there are two such categories. They may be called deliberate and involuntary, or mortal and venial. Each has its appropriate remedy. The second corollary is that Christians can be divided into two classes: spiritual Christians, who live in godly fear of mortal sin, continually seeking sanctification by repentance of venial sins and indifferent Christians who live in peril of grave lapses, and have hope of salvation only through the ministrations of the Church.[8]

The doctrine of Second Repentance, and the procedures for administering it, developed throughout the third century, fueled by two particular problems. First was the problem of general immorality, especially unchastity within the Church. Second, the Church wrestled with the problem of those who lapsed during times of persecution, and then sought readmittance to the community when it was again safe. The latter problem became especially acute in North Africa after the Decian persecution of 249. Each step the Church took toward leniency was met with an angry response by the rigorists whose protest often led them into schism or heresy.

Montanism was, for example, a rigorist movement that

favored strict ecclesiastical discipline to foster the ideal of holiness. Montanists feared that granting forgiveness to notorious sinners might encourage others to sin. Its most notable voice was that of Tertullian who, after he became a Montanist, sought very strict limits to any Second Repentance and argued that some sins, such as idolatry, murder, and adultery, were actually unforgivable. Cyprian of Carthage, a generation later, confronted the problem of the lapsed and sought to make provisions for readmitting the truly penitent, while avoiding excessive laxity. His was the approach of a bishop and pastor confronting human frailty. In addition to Tertullian and Cyprian, many of the finest minds of the early Patristic period wrestled with the problem of Second Repentance, among them Irenaeus, Clement of Alexandria, and Origen.[9]

With the Peace of Constantine, in the early fourth century, the Church entered a new era in which its penitential discipline was characterized by the flowering of classical "canonical (public) penance." A horde of new converts threatened the moral integrity of the Christian community, and canonical penance developed through conciliar decisions, papal decretals, collections of private directions, and "penitential letters." Through its use several ends were achieved, at least in theory. Sinners were led to see the terrible actuality of their status before God and the community, and the community's standards were thus upheld. Penance was a medicine to exorcise the evil from the sinner and an expression of sorrow and apology to God and the Church. The congregation was an integral part of the process, and canonical penance enlisted their prayers, sorrow, and action on behalf of sinners in their midst.[10]

In general, the process of canonical penance worked as follows. The notorious sinner, upon realizing the danger of his or her sin, would approach the community through the bishop and ask for permission to do penance. If admitted, the penitent was enrolled in the order of penitents and excluded from the communion of the Church. Penitents often stood in a special place, such as the back of the church, and were dismissed along with the catechumens at the Offering or before the Prayers of the Faithful. Frequently, they were clothed in a special garment, the goatskin *cilicium*, and their hair was cropped. During the term of their penance, they were required to renounce all pleasures and required to perform acts of mortification, such as curtailment of sleep, abstinence from conjugal relations, and the renunciation of worldly honors. They confessed the sins that had brought them to penance, either publicly or privately. During the liturgy, the congregation prayed for them, and hands were laid on them while they knelt.

The term of penance might be as little as forty days or as long as many years, depending on the judgment of the bishop as to the severity of the sin. When the term was ended and the bishop satisfied, penitents were reconciled by episcopal blessing, the laying-on of hands, and readmission to communion. The ministry of canonical penance was reserved to the bishop, although as time went on it was increasingly delegated to presbyters. Canonical penance could be performed only once, and the reconciled penitent was committed to a lifetime of self-denial and ascetic discipline.[11]

It is to the writings of St. Augustine of Hippo that we owe much of our knowledge about the theory and practice of canonical penance. His theology of penance, related to his development of the notion of "original sin" and the working of God's grace, served to alter the attitude of later generations regarding sin and forgiveness. Previously, the Church had been concerned with actual sins that human effort could overcome. Now, she began to recognize that only God can make human beings good, even after baptism erases the effects of original sin. The baptized person retains the bias toward evil that makes sin inevitable. Augustine divided such sin into two categories: *peccata*, which occur daily and for which we daily repent by the offering of "better deeds," and *crimina*, which cause a fall from grace and can only be dealt with by canonical penance. With Augustine, the distinction between venial and mortal sin becomes more precise, and the view of the Church is less the "company of the saints" than an "ark for the perishing." This had a significant bearing on the further development of the Church's penitential discipline.[12]

By the sixth century, several factors were making the continuation of canonical penance increasingly less possible and were preparing the way for new developments. First, there was the severity of canonical penance, and the life-long disabilities incurred by those who chose it. Since penance could be done only once and sentenced one to the renunciation of the "life of the world," more and more Christians put it off until their deathbeds. Indeed, penance changed from being an extraordinary measure taken in the case of grave sin to a common preparation for the death of the devout. Penance also became ritualized, as it was increasingly used in Lent with the whole congregation participating often in the disciplines. Further, the period saw the rise of monasticism and the "religious life" whose rigors were remarkably like penance. Parallel to this was the development of the *conversi*, laypersons undertaking a life of penance out of piety rather than sin. Finally, the monastic movement gave rise to the mutual confession of sins as a therapeutic practice for those who sought perfection. The practice of seeking out a "spiritual father" for the confession of venial sins was commended in Benedict's *Rule* and the *Pastoral Care* of Gregory the Great. The abandonment of canonical penance by the ordinary sinner and the cultivation of confession and ascetic discipline by the devout doomed the older institution to extinction.[13]

It may be useful to summarize some of the principal themes of our discussion of the early Church and Patristic periods, not only because these themes will continue to appear in subsequent history, but because much contemporary liturgical scholarship and theology seeks to recover earlier understandings of the forgiveness of sins that have been obscured by later developments. Reconciliation was, in the earliest days of the Church, intimately associated with Baptism, which was understood to be the sacrament of forgiveness *par excellence*. As the early Church's baptismal discipline faded away, so did this intimate connection with reconciliation. Although penance was always intimately linked with the Eucharist, the Church's understanding of that linkage was increasingly individualized. No longer was the concern so much to maintain the integrity of the eucharistic assembly as to make sure that individual Christians made "worthy" communions.

The more ancient eschatological and corporate dimensions of reconciliation were also transformed. The notion of the forgiveness of sins as the sign of the breaking-in of the Kingdom was diluted more and more as the Church's life became stable and institutionalized. The notion that the community is the locus of the Church's penitential discipline was largely lost as the Church became more hierarchical, and what had been a corporate obligation became a priestly prerogative.

Finally, penance became more and more juridical, both in its administration and in its theological rationale. The next periods of history were to see a legalistic approach to the three parts that had evolved: the confession, the penance, and the reconciliation. Finally, the old rough-and-ready distinctions between more and less serious sins yielded to rigid distinctions between mortal and venial sins, and the whole science of casuistry developed. Not all of the changes were necessarily bad in themselves, but we will note the effort of contemporary theologians to recover earlier understandings as part of their efforts at sacramental renewal in the twentieth century.

The Early Middle Ages

The decline of canonical public penance, despite the best efforts of bishops and councils, left a void in the Church's life that cried out to be filled. The problem of post-baptismal sin had hardly disappeared and, despite the heroic piety of monastic communities, the ordinary Christian still stood in need of actualized reconciliation. As Gunstone puts it,

> What the Church needed was a disciplinary system under which the penitent could be reconciled as often as he was truly repentant and which allowed him to resume normal life again afterwards. She needed to be able to forgive not once but seventy times seven.[14]

What emerged is most readily described as "private penance," aptly defined by Mortimer:

> By private penance is meant a penance other than the formal public penance of those "who are properly called penitents," "who have done penance in the *cilicium* and been subsequently reconciled to the Altar." Above all is meant a penance to which recourse may be had any number of times in a lifetime, and which involved no permanent disabilities. Provided that there was a priestly absolu-

tion, that a second penance was possible, and that the absolved penitent was able to resume his normal occupation, then, no matter what degree of publicity attached to the absolution of his penance, there we have a private penitential system.[15]

Although its origins are shrouded in obscurity, there seems little doubt that private penance was a peculiar creation of the Celtic Church, which owed a remarkable measure of independence to its geographical isolation. Celtic penitential discipline seems to have its roots in the pre-Christian institution of the *anmchara*, or "soul friend," a guide of souls who heard confessions and gave authoritative counsel.[16] Such a figure was natural to the Celtic Church, which tended to be tribal and monastic rather than territorial and hierarchical.

The "soul friends" and confessors of the Irish Church developed books that specified the appropriate penance for each sin. These enabled the confessor to deal with sin without recourse to the local bishop. They established a principle of proportionality and tended to be quite comprehensive. The Celtic Penitentials, as these books were called, were characterized by a deep moral earnestness and were admirably designed to impress upon a half-converted and barbarian people the basic demands of justice and personal morality. The typical penances were fasting, prayer, alms-giving, and various ascetic disciplines. What is sometimes known as "tariff penance" became part of a system that included various remissions, redemptions, and shortenings. For example, a longer period of moderate penitential discipline could be replaced by a shorter period of greater severity, or even by an appropriate level of almsgiving. Although the system was subject to abuses, it worked well, and the Penitentials spread throughout the British Isles. They were uncanonical and depended for their acceptance on the reputation of their alleged authors. In short, they were examples of a true grass-roots reform.[17]

The spread of the Celtic Penitentials went hand in hand with the advance of law and order in Anglo-Saxon territories. Thomas P. Oakely made a very interesting study of the relationship of the Penitentials to the development of Anglo-Saxon law and discovered a symbiotic relationship between the Church and the state on the frontier of civilization. He concluded:

It will be readily seen that the penitential system and secular laws mutually assisted each other in punishing criminals and in working for the preservation of law and order. The secular laws, on their part, offered substantial aid to the introduction and enforcement of confession and penance by providing severe penalties for their neglect and by alleviating secular penalties for those who performed them. On the other hand, the Church severely penanced those who neglected or resisted the enforcement of secular penalties; it insisted upon respect for the procedure of the secular courts; and, in many ways, it held up to detestation crimes and criminals. The chief *media* of the Church for this important work were the Penitentials.[18]

Thus were the barbarians converted and civilized.

There were at this time innumerable barbarians on the continent in need of conversion and civilization, and much of this work was accomplished by the monk-missionaries of the Celtic and Anglo-Saxon Church. These heroic ecclesiastical pioneers took the Penitentials, and the institution of private (tariff) penance, with them. By the year 1000, this system had so spread that many Western Christians accepted its appropriateness and antiquity. The hierarchy in lands where the faith had been longer established might rant and rail against this innovation, and rant and rail they did, but it was an accomplished fact. As Mortimer puts it,

And with this simple yet far-reaching reform the lesser sins which so easily beset us were brought within the normal sphere of penance, and the grace and comfort of absolution, no longer limited to the very wicked or heroic, was continuously bestowed upon the ordinary humble and devout Christian.[19]

By the thirteenth century, this was the situation. Public penance was still in effect, but rarely practiced and only for the gravest and most scandalous cases. Priestly absolution was seen increasingly in sacramental terms and "expressed the Church's belief in her own authority and also in the efficacy of her prayers, especially the prayers of the saints."[20] As a development of the old monastic practice, the "confession of devotion" had spread as part of the normal life of the devout. All this was formally recognized by the Church at the Fourth Lateran Council of 1213 in its decree requiring an annual, pre-Easter *private* confession. The reform was complete, and Reconciliation had attained the form it was to have for the next several centuries in the West.

Schoolmen and Reformers

While Lateran IV had settled the issue of the practice of private penance, its theoretical foundation had not developed to any great extent. This was the work of the High Middle Ages, the great flowering of scholastic theology. The rite of penance gave scholastic theologians a fit topic on which to exercise their argumentation, and they embraced the topic energetically. Two urgent questions presented themselves. What was the intrinsic relationship of the different aspects of the rite to each other? And, how was penance to be understood as a sacrament, what was its "matter" and what its "form"? Peter Lombard had placed penance among the Seven Sacraments, but what precisely did that mean? Then, too, there was considerable debate over the distinction between *contrition*, the deep sorrow for sin that all agreed merited God's forgiveness, and *attrition*, a fear of punishment, or a less than complete contrition. Did attrition merit absolution? And what, exactly, did that priestly absolution mean?[21]

It would be inaccurate to say that the Angelic Doctor, St. Thomas Aquinas, settled all these questions, but he did provide a basic framework for understanding. This framework was made normative by the Council of Trent, and its use persisted in the Roman Catholic Church until Vatican II. Aquinas held that the three "parts" of the sacrament—contrition, confession, and satisfaction— were the *matter* and that the absolution was the *form*. Efficacy derived from the form and the signification of the sacrament from the matter. The absolution communicated the fruits of Christ's passion to the penitent, as the penitent cooperated with grace in the destruction of sin. Coming to confession is a sign of the sinner's will to be converted, and Aquinas taught that the absolution could change attrition to contrition and thus positively effect the forgiveness of sin. Fr. Poschmann summarizes,

The great and epoch-making achievement of Aquinas' teaching on penance was the integration of the sacrament in the process of justification, and consequently the proof that it was an indispensible cause of the forgiveness of sin.[22]

The theologians engaged in considerable further debate on the subject of penance, but Thomism gradually won out and represents the height of the Scholastic achievement up to the time of the Reformation.[23]

By asserting so positively the sacramental power of the Church to pronounce forgiveness *ex opere operato* in the absolution, the issue was much clarified, but the door was also opened to many abuses. Given the supreme importance of the forgiveness of sins and reconciliation with God in Christ to the faith, it is not surprising that this very issue touched off the Protestant Reformation. Indeed, the first two of Luther's Ninety-five Theses attacked the very institution of sacramental penance, denying that it was what the Lord meant when he said, "Repent!" Luther proclaimed instead that only faith enables men and women to appropriate the righteousness God gracefully attributes to them in Christ.

Luther did not necessarily intend to abolish confession, but he saw it from a pastoral, rather than juridical, point of view. He denied that it was a sacrament of the Gospel, and considered it valuable chiefly in quieting the troubled conscience. For him, the absolution was declaratory; it proclaimed that God forgives all human sin through Christ. The true work of the confessor, therefore, is to evoke and strengthen faith, a faith that will assure the devout Christian who is *simul justus et peccator* (at once righteous and a sinner), that he is saved by Christ alone.[24]

Luther set forth a form of confession in the *Small Catechism*, as we shall see later, and the idea of voluntary confession never quite died out in later Lutheranism. It was rarely used, however, and tended in practice to be superseded by preaching, pastoral care through visitation, and the mutual care of souls by groups of the devout laity. Further, the very way in which Luther dealt with confession as assurance could give rise to a rather subjective treatment of Reconciliation.

Thus, against such an ecclesiastical transaction as the so-called Sacrament of Penance, the Augsburg Confession made canonical the Lutheran "evangelical experience" ("we know ourselves forgiven when we believe ourselves to be the objects of divine favor in Christ") and so asserted something that was in danger of becoming subjective, unless all weight were thrown upon the abiding word of Scripture.[25]

Other reformers gave confession even shorter shrift and tended to eliminate any kind of absolution byond the merely declaratory. In Calvin's Geneva something like the old public penance was administered by the civil magistrates, and divine worship contained a general confession of sin and a declaration of pardon. Calvin regarded private confession, either to a pastor or to a fellow-Christian, as something salutary but by no means necessary. Confession might be valuable for the correction of the sinner, the quieting of an uneasy conscience, or reconciliation among Christians, but Calvin did not regard it as in any way sacramental. For Zwingli, frequent confession to God is an integral part of the Christian life; but confession to another Christian, except for the purpose of advice, is of no particular value. In time, the subjective "evangelical experience" was transmuted by the radical reformation into something very like today's experience of "being born again." This was especially true when it was combined with the Calvinist concern with discerning the assurance of one's election. The priestly ministry of absolution would find no place in this sort of piety or theology.[26]

The Council of Trent rejected any compromise with the Reformation and emphasized penance as a true sacrament. It proclaimed the necessity of confession and its divine institution as deriving from the power of the keys. Absolution was held to be a judicial act and not merely declaratory, and the Thomist view that the sacrament of penance was the efficient cause of the forgiveness of sins was canonized. The Council also set forth a *Rite of Penance* incorporating this view which, with minor modifications, was used in the Roman Catholic Church until the liturgical reforms of the Second Vatican Council. Thus, Christendom remained divided for four hundred years over the essential matter of reconciliation with God in Christ.[27]

Reconciliation in Anglicanism

Since this is an unabashedly Anglican work, we now turn our

attention to the English Reformation and the history of Reconciliation in the Church of England and her daughter churches. A
short description of what we may take to be typical pre-Reforma-
tion English practice will set the scene. John Mirk, a member of an
Augustinian community in Shropshire, wrote a small work
entitled *Instructions for Parish Priests*, which had a wide circulation
in the fourteenth and fifteenth centuries. Half of it consisted of
instructions to a "shrift father" (that is, one who shrives, or hears
confessions).

According to Mirk, one ought normally to make one's confession to one's own parish priest. He is to examine the penitent to
see whether he or she knows the Paternoster, the Ave Maria, and
the Creed. The priest examines the penitent according to the Ten
Commandments, seeking specificity. He should never impose a
heavy penance, so as to discourage the penitent, and should,
when possible, urge the penitent to the practice of the appropriate
virtue, e.g., acts of humility for the proud. Apparently, the confession was heard in the nave; no special furniture was normally
used before the Reformation.[28] Here we see the homely, familiar,
pastoral approach that has characterized the best in English practice.

The English Reformation was, from the beginning, characterized by a kind of tug-of-war between a conservatism that wanted
a moderate reform, and the more radical Lutheran and,
especially, Calvinist doctrines. The Elizabethan Settlement was
anti-Catholic, but not necessarily pro-Calvinist, although Cal-
vinism, in its Puritan form, did leave its mark on *The Book of
Common Prayer* and the Thirty-nine Articles of Religion. The pull
of these various tendencies clearly can be seen in the succession of
Prayer Books from 1549, through 1552 (and the Elizabethan
restoration of 1559), and finally to 1662. Since *The Book of Common
Prayer* is the primary source for all Anglican liturgical theology, we
turn now to it to explore the Church of England's understanding
of Reconciliation.[29]

In the more "Protestant" book of 1552, a General Confession
was added at beginning of Morning and Evening Prayer (Mattins
and Evensong), using an essentially Genevan form with a declaratory absolution. The absolution was to be pronounced by "the

minister," but in the rubric of 1662 the office was given to "the priest," upon whom the ordination rites of 1552 and 1662 quite explicitly confer the power of the keys.[30] The confession at Holy Communion, identical in all three Books, was non-Calvinist and the absolution rather conservative.[31]

In the office for the Visitation of the Sick, the priest is enjoined to urge the sick person to confess any troubling sins, and provided an absolution that combines a prayer that God will forgive the sin with an out-and-out authoritative absolution, includiing the "I absolve thee" formulation canonized at Trent:

> Our Lord Jesus Christ, who hath left power to his Church to absolve sinners who truly repent and believe in him, of his great mercy forgive thee thine offences: and by his authority committed to me, I absolve thee from all thy sins in the name of the Father, and of the Son, and of the Holy Ghost. Amen.

In the 1549 Prayer Book, the rubric that introduces this absolution directs that the same form be used "in all private confessions." While that rubric was removed from subsequent Prayer Books, this absolution has been consistently used in private confessions in Anglicanism ever since.[38]

The Anglican position on private confession was spelled out most clearly in the Exhortation, included with the Holy Communion in the 1549 *Book of Common Prayer*:

> And if there be any of you whose conscience is troubled and grieved in anything, lacking comfort or counsel, let him come to me, or to some other discreet and learned priest taught in the law of God, and confess and open his sin and grief secretly, that he may receive such ghostly counsel, advice and comfort that his conscience may be relieved, and that of us, as the ministers of God and of the church, he may receive comfort and absolution, to the satisfaction of his mind and avoiding of all scruple and doubtfulness: requiring such as shall be satisifed with a general confession not to be offended with them that do use to their further satisfying the auricular and secret confession to the priest; nor those also which think needful or convenient, for the quietness of their own consciences, particularly to open their sins to the priest, to be offended with them that are satisfied with their humble confession to God and the general confession to the church: but in all things follow and keep the rule of charity, and every man to be satisfied with his

own conscience, not judging other men's minds or consciences whereas he hath no warrant of God's Word to the same.

The 1552 revision altered the Exhortation to the form it retained subsequently:

> And because it is requisite that no man should come to the Holy Communion but with a full trust in God's mercy, and with a quiet conscience, therefore if there be any of you which by the means aforesaid cannot quiet his own conscience, but requireth further comfort or counsel; then let him come to me, or some other discreet and learned minister of God's word and open his grief that he may receive such ghostly counsel, advice and comfort as his conscience may be relieved and that by the ministry of God's Word he receive comfort and the benefit of absolution, to the quieting of his conscience, and avoiding of all scruple and doubtfulness.[33]

Thus, a non-obligatory confession with absolution was retained by the reformed Church of England for the benefit of those in need. The Exhortations, and especially that of 1549, are the root of the old Anglican maxim about auricular confession: all may, none must, some should.

The English reformers also attempted to restore public penance as a means of discipline in the Church. The Commination, to be used on Ash Wednesday, begins with an exhortation describing the penitential discipline of the primitive Church and stating that portions of Scripture describing God's wrath should be read, "until the said discipline may be restored again (which thing is much to be wished)."[34] The Thirty-nine Articles and the Canons of 1604 recognized greater and lesser forms of excommunication, and there is some evidence of various forms of public penance being practiced in parish churches into the early nineteenth century. Public penance remained a decided oddity in the Church of England, however, as it had throughout the West after the sixth century.[35]

The basic teaching of the Prayer Book and the Articles was defended in the seventeenth century by that illustrious group of theologians known collectively as the Caroline Divines. In their concern to answer the polemics of both the Roman Catholics and the Puritans, they formulated a theory of private confession. They located their doctrine in the scriptural definition of repentance as a state of the soul related to the demands of ordinary Christian living and the quest for personal holiness. They denied that ritual repentance was a sacrament ordained by Christ himself, and yet affirmed it as a sacramental act. They were suspicious of the distinction between venial and mortal sins, holding that all sin is serious. They saw the outward manifestations of fasting, prayer, alms, and good deeds as the fruits of repentance, but not the repentance itself. They rejected the Scholastic notion of expiatory satisfaction, for, after all, in the words of the Prayer Book, Christ on the Cross made a "full, perfect and sufficient sacrifice, oblation and satisfaction for the sins of the whole world." They recognized, however, that the penitent must cooperate with grace to receive the benefits of that sacrifice. Finally, they rejected any requirement for auricular confession as unscriptural, but did not seek to discourage those who wished it.1316

Richard Hooker was typical of the Carolines, and Book VI of his *Laws of Ecclesiastical Polity* deals with the forgiveness of sins. He set forth as a prime pastoral duty the teaching of self-examination before communion, and he held that the procedure described in the Exhortation could be useful in overcoming scrupulousness. The Church's duty is to make people sorry for their sins, but to assure them at the same time of God's mercy. The priest says, "I absolve thee" not as a judge but as a pastoral response to the grief of the believer over his or her sins. Christian life, for Hooker, is a growth in faith and holiness, and thus a growth in penitence. In this growth the Church has a primary role, and the offering of absolution to the penitent is part of that role; it is efficacious in that for which it was ordained.[37] Hooker provides an admirable summary of the Carolines' teaching on Confession:

> The minister's power to absolve is publicly taught and professed, the Church not denied to have authority either of abridging or enlarging the use and exercise of that power, upon the people no such necessity imposed of opening their transgressions unto men, as if remission of sins otherwise were impossible; neither any such opinion had of the thing itself, as though it were either unlawful or unprofitable, saving only for these inconveniences, which the world hath by experience observed in it heretofore. And in regard thereof, the Church of England hitherto hath thought it the safer way to refer men's hidden crimes unto God and themselves only; howbeit,

not without special caution for the admonition of such as come to
the holy Sacrament, and for the comfort of such as are ready to
depart the world.[38]

English reformers and apologists argued for the value of
private confession, offered in the Prayer Book, but provided no
form for it. There is evidence that some made use of the opportunity through the end of the seventeenth century. Hooker confessed on his deathbed, and until around 1700, Confessors to the
Royal Household were appointed. Non-Jurors and High Church-
men took a high view of absolution and commended the practice.
Nonetheless, there is little evidence to suggest that from 1700 on
private confession in the Church of England was anything more
than a theoretical possibility and so unusual as to be remarkable
when it occurred.[39]

In the mid-nineteenth century, however, the revival of sacramental confession became one of the notable aims of the Oxford
Movement and the Anglo-Catholic party. This effort was one of
the most controversial aspects of a very controversial movement.
However, as Tractarian influence spread, so did the practice of
confession. In 1877, after some hesitation, Pusey published a
translation and adaptation of the Abbé Jean Joseph Gaume's
Manual for Confessors. In the United States, followers of Pusey and
his colleagues, such as J. O. S. Huntington, founder of the Order
of the Holy Cross, sought to revive the cure of souls through the
confessional.[40]

Opposition was vigorous from the Evangelical wing of the
Church, however, and in the nineteenth and early twentieth century, the opposition was in the majority. In 1877, the Convocation
of Canterbury resolved sixty-two to six that:

> The Church of England, in the Twenty-Fifth Article, affirms that
> penance is not to be counted as a sacrament of the Gospel; and, as
> judged by her formularies, knows no such words as "sacramental
> confession."[41]

The Lambeth Conference of 1878 sought to express the mind of
the whole Anglican Communion on the subject by unanimously
endorsing these words:

> ... It is [our] deliberate opinion that no minister of the Church is

authorized to require from those who may resort to him to open their grief a particular or detailed enumeration of all their sins, or to require private confession previous to receiving the Holy Communion, or to enjoin or *even encourage* the practice of habitual confession to a priest or to teach that such practice of habitual confession, or the being subject to what has been termed the direction of a priest, is a condition of attaining the highest spiritual life. At the same time [we] are not to be understood as desiring to limit in any way the provision made in the Book of Common Prayer for the relief of troubled consciences.[48]

According to this view, vigorously argued by John Stott in *Confess Your Sins*, so-called sacramental confession is only a remedy for extraordinary situations. Any more frequent practice is unscriptural and unnecessary. Confession should be made directly to God, to the persons one has offended, and to the community for violations of its standards. His version of the old maxim would seem to be, "all may, none must, none should."

In this controversy, viewed from the latter part of the twentieth century, neither the deep-dyed Anglo-Catholic nor the red-hot Evangelical has entirely won. Participation in the Reconciliation of a Penitent has become an unremarkable feature of the piety of many Anglicans, but the crowds are not exactly beating down the doors to the confessional. American Episcopalians have two forms for the rite, but there is no evidence to suggest either vigorous controversy or widespread use. There has been a revival of sorts, but it touches only those who choose to be touched by it. In short it seems safe to say that private confession in the Anglican Communion in the 1980s remains what it has been for several hundred years—a homely, pastoral meeting of some of the faithful with their priests, in which the forgiving love of God is made known in a special way. John Gunstone, in his marvelous little book *The Liturgy of Penance*, puts it very well:

Going to confession in the Church of England is to take part in one of the most informal of all liturgical acts. Although the lack of common discipline and canonical directions about private penance has its disadvantages, this has to be set against the free and fruitful relationship between confessor and penitent which is a characteristic of Anglicanism. The liturgy of penance has become a purely pastoral instrument of individual care.[43]

III

Contemporary Rites
of Reconciliation

HAVING completed our historical survey, we are now in a position to look at various rites of reconciliation in use today in several traditions, and then to attempt an ecumenical synthesis of the theology of the rites. Specifically, we will analyze the orders for reconciliation in the American *Book of Common Prayer* (1979), the Roman Catholic *Rite of Penance* (1973), and *The Lutheran Book of Worship* (1978). We will discuss briefly the status of sacramental confession in other churches, as well. I believe that we can find a substantial consensus as to the meaning of this rite or sacrament across these various traditions. Further, I believe that our ability to do this points up two very important facts about our enterprise: today's ecumenical context, and the close relationship between liturgy and doctrine, or theology and praxis.

It is a commonplace that we live in an increasingly ecumenical age, one marked by a far greater respect and sharing among various Christian groups than has obtained since the Reformation. This is especially true in the related disciplines of liturgical scholarship and sacramental theology. The origins of this trend lie in the early twentieth century and, in our particular area, are evidenced by, for example, the Protestant Max Thurian's splendid work on confession with its great appreciation of Roman Catholicism deriving from the Taizé community, and the Franciscan Stephan Richter's enthusiastic appreciation for Protestant developments and his efforts to rehabilitate Luther as a good Catholic, at least with respect to his views on confession.[1] Indeed, there seems to be a revival of interest in Luther among Roman Catholics; we find scholars arguing that the essential aspects of the great reformer's objections to mediaeval penance were articulated by the bishops at the Council of Trent![2] Thus, the matter of sacramental reconciliation, which played a major role in starting the Reformation, is also very much a part of efforts to repair some of the wounds in the Body of Christ that resulted from it.

Liturgical reform and revision is now done ecumenically. Most churches no longer revise their liturgical books or refine their theology of worship and the sacraments in a vacuum. Sources, ideas, processes, and texts themselves are increasingly shared acrosss denominational lines. In all of this, a central position must be given to the Liturgical Movement in the Roman Catholic Church, which was crowned by the massive revision of all its rites as a result of the Second Vatican Council in the early 1960s. Vatican II has been a catalyst for liturgical and theological development in the Anglican and Lutheran families, and indeed throughout "mainstream" Protestantism. In the past two decades, all these churches have revised their liturgies along remarkably similar lines.[3]

The second factor that deserves our close attention is the relationship between liturgy and theology, worship and belief, sacramental forms and Christian life. We have seen historically how the development of rites of penance influenced the Church's understanding of the forgiveness of sins and vice versa. This obeys the great maxim *lex orandi, lex credendi*, the law of prayer is the law of belief. Certainly, this is basic to Anglicanism, which has always maintained *The Book of Common Prayer* as its central doctrinal, as well as liturgical, document. In the Episcopal Church, the revisers of the Prayer Book, as well as its apologists and opponents, have agreed that the new services are intended to reflect, and engender, new understandings and expressions of the faith. This has been true throughout the whole history of the Church, and is well expressed by Monika Hellwig:

> The first observation one makes in looking at this history and trying to understand it is that there is such a strong reciprocity between the praxis of forgiving and reconciling and the theoretical understanding of God's forgiveness. Each constantly conditions the other.[4]

With all this in mind, let us turn to the rites themselves. Our interest will be not so much in the texts, though we will need to consider them, but in the theological understandings they embody.

The Book of Common Prayer (1979)

The various rites in the present *Book of Common Prayer* (*BCP* 1979) of the Episcopal Church witness to the centrality of the forgiveness of sins in the Gospel and to our human condition as sinners.[5] Although the penitential emphasis is not as marked as in previous Anglican Prayer Books, it is nonetheless undeniably present and pervasive. Rather, there is a greater balance in the expression of these two dialectical elements: human sin and divine mercy. The Anglican tradition of acknowledging and confessing sin in corporate worship has been retained fully. There is penitential material in most services, and, indeed, in some in which it had not been included previously, e.g., the offices for marriage and burial.[6]

The daily offices have penitential beginnings, as they have had since 1552, as do the two rites for the Holy Eucharist. These latter also have an order for confession and absolution within them. At Morning and Evening Prayer, as well as at the Eucharist, the confession of sin is followed by a prayer for forgiveness (if the officiant is a layperson or a deacon) or an absolution by a priest. Confession and forgiveness is not relegated to a special rite but incorporated into the public worship of the Church as a normal practice.

In the Outline of the Faith, further statement of these themes is very prominent. The Catechism begins with a statement about "Human Nature" that recognizes our sinfulness (p. 845). There is a section on "Sin and Redemption" that introduces the section on God the Son and describes redemption as "the act of God which sets us free from the power of evil, sin and death" (p. 849). The importance of Jesus' suffering and death is that, "By his obedience . . . Jesus made the offering which we could not make; in him we are freed from the power of sin and reconciled to God"

(p. 850). The theme of reconciliation is made central to the Catechism's doctrine of the Church, whose mission is "to restore all people to unity with God and each other in Christ" (p. 855). Each order of ministry is charged with carrying on Christ's work of reconciliation, and this includes the laity (pp. 855–56). Penitence is listed as one of the principal kinds of prayer and defined as the confession of sins, the making of restitution where possible, and the intention to amend our lives (p. 857). Among the benefits of the Lord's Supper are the forgiveness of sins, and when we come to the Eucharist, "It is required that we should examine our lives, repent of our sins, and be in love and charity with all people" (pp. 859–60). There seems to be little question that, for Episcopalians, Jesus' ministry of forgiveness and reconciliation is central to our understanding of who he is, and who Christians are as the Body of Christ.

While the ministry of Reconciliation is clearly the task of the whole Church, the Prayer Book and the practice of the Episcopal Church assigns a special ministry to presbyters and bishops. Laypersons are, according to the Catechism, "to carry on Christ's work of reconciliation" (p. 855). Bishops, on the other hand, are to "act in Christ's name for the reconciliation of the world," and presbyters are "to bless and pardon in the name of God" (pp. 855–56). There is, therefore, a special authority and responsibility committed to these ordained ministers to act on behalf of the Lord and his Church. This is fully consistent with an Anglican theology of ordination, ever since the very first Prayer Books in which presbyters were quite explicitly given the power of the keys at ordination. In the 1979 Ordinal, the bishop charges the ordinand "to declare God's forgiveness to penitent sinners" (p. 531), and the rubrics reserve to bishops and priests the authoritative pronouncement of forgiveness in all rites. The *BCP* 1979, makes it quite clear, however, that the power and authority to do this comes from God, through the Church by delegation.

The authoritative proclamation of forgiveness is made in several ways which, in the light of history, serve to illuminate the Episcopal Church's intent and understanding. We may discern three forms of forgiveness-pronouncements, or absolutions: precatory (or deprecatory), declaratory, and authoritative (or indicative).[7] The precatory form is a prayer that the penitent(s) will be forgiven. It is an expression of eschatological hope and looks forward to accomplishment in the Kingdom. This was the form most common in the early Church. In the declaratory form, the Church proclaims that the forgiveness of sins is a fact because of the redeeming work of Christ. This is a realized eschatology, an expression of trust and faith in the presence of the Kingdom now. This form, based as it is on an emphasis of the grace of God, is that most favored by the churches of the Reformation. Even today, most Protestant orders of worship follow a confession with a "declaration (or assurance) of pardon" in general terms. The authoritative form of pronouncement is a concrete statement that this particular penitent is forgiven his or her sins. In the "I absolve you" form, the Word is proclaimed in the present tense with specificity. This is the form that came to be used in Western Catholicism and was vigorously defended at Trent.

All three forms have theological and historical validity as expressions of varying emphases of the one Christian faith. They are, respectively, eschatological, kerygmatic, and incarnational in thrust. Although the nuances of their use have been the source of much controversy over the centuries, a full liturgical expression of the Christian Gospel will include them all. This is, in fact, what we find in *The Book of Common Prayer* 1979, and it stands, on this point, in historical continuity with all previous Prayer Books.

There is no pure representative of these forms in the *BCP*; all are mixed, but with differing emphases. The standard Rite II form, used at both the offices and the Eucharist, is in the subjunctive mood and seems to carry an authoritative sense in a precatory form:

> Almighty God have mercy on you, forgive you all your sins through our Lord Jesus Christ, strengthen you in all goodness, and by the power of the Holy Spirit keep you in eternal life.

The absolution in Holy Eucharist Rite I, which comes from previous Prayer Books, combines an authoritative statement in a declaratory form:

> Almighty God, our heavenly Father, who of his great mercy hath promised forgiveness of sins to all those who with hearty repen-

tance and true faith turn unto him, have mercy upon you, pardon and deliver you from all your sins, confirm and strengthen you in all goodness, and bring you to everlasting life. (p. 332)

The older form of absolution at Morning and Evening Prayer has been preserved for use on Ash Wednesday and is close to being purely declaratory (p. 269). The clearest statement in the authoritative form, with a declaratory preface, comes from the 1549 Visitation order and is used in the Reconciliation of a Penitent.

When we turn to the two forms for Reconciliation (pp. 447ff.), we find rites of individual confession and absolution similar in many respects to that of the post-Tridentine Roman Catholic Church. They are clearly in historical continuity with the Western tradition of auricular confession. We cannot thereby assume, however, that the Episcopal Church has simply accepted the theological position of Roman Catholicism; any knowledge of Anglican tradition would discourage us from that error. We are also immediately aware of the Anglican Church's maddening habit of rarely explaining the meaning of its rites in any detail. To understand what the Church intends these forms to do will require careful reading of the rites themselves and further research in the Prayer Book.

Two clues are provided by the Catechism and the placement of the Reconciliation of a Penitent. The former classifies Reconciliation as one of the "other sacramental rites," which means that it is a "means of grace, [but] not necessary for all persons in the same way that Baptism and the Eucharist are" (p. 860). It is also called Penance and "is the rite in which those who repent of their sins may confess them to God in the presence of a priest, and receive the assurance of pardon and the grace of absolution" (p. 861). It is placed in the Prayer Book in the section containing "Pastoral Offices," which, in the words of Marion Hatchett, "contains rites which mark significant turning points (crises) in the lives of individuals within the community."[8] That they are for individuals does not render them "private," however. As Hatchett observes, they are a part of community concern, and some are to be celebrated publicly. The pastoral Offices are those rites used in the ministry of the Church to persons in particular need. Thus, by

their placement, the forms of Reconciliation are pastoral in intent,
and not juridical.

The rites are prefaced with a few statements that help indicate
their meaning and how they should be administered. These comments begin with the assertion that:

> The ministry of reconciliation, which has been committed by Christ
> to his Church, is exercised through the care each Christian has for
> others, through the common prayer of Christians assembled for
> public worship, and through the priesthood of the Church and its
> ministers declaring absolution (p. 446).

Therefore, the rite is voluntary for Episcopalians, being *a*
means by which Reconciliation occurs in the Church. Further, the
authority for Reconciliation resides in the corporate priesthood of
the Church, which acts through ordained ministers. Absolution,
as such, is limited to bishops and presbyters, although, in accord
with ancient practice and Reformation understanding, ordinary
Christians can hear each other's confessions. As in Roman Catholic practice, the seal of the confession, its confidentiality, is absolute.

In another significant statement, we read that when "the
penitent has confessed all serious sins troubling the conscience
and has given evidence of due contrition, the priest gives such
counsel and encouragement as needed and pronounces absolution" (p. 446). We see here a balancing of the Reformation
Anglican stress on confession for the relief of uneasy conscience
with the historical use of the rite for serious sins. No distinction of
mortal and venial sins is made, however; the subject does not arise.
"Evidence of due contrition" is sufficient for the absolution and
no "satisfaction" is required, although "the priest may assign to the
penitent a psalm, prayer or hymn to be said, or something to be
done, as a sign of penitence and an act of thanksgiving" (p. 446).
The rites are placed next to Ministry to the Sick, which is historically apt, but the introductory rubrics point out that Reconciliation is available at any time, not just when a Christian is sick.[9]
Great flexibility is given the priest and penitent as to how the
confession will be heard.

Form One of the Reconciliation of a Penitent is what one

might call an Anglicanized adaptation of the older Roman rite and is very similar to the typical adaptation made by the Tractarians and other Anglo-Catholic manuals in the last century, with certain "Romish" touches excised.[10] It is similar to orders for confession found in other provinces of the Anglican Communion. Two absolutions are given, the first a contemporary language version from the 1549 Visitation office and the second drafted from a form approved by the Roman Consilium of Vatican II by Massey Shepherd.[11] In Form One, the penitent asks for and receives a blessing from the priest and confesses his or her sins. The priest "may offer counsel, direction and comfort" and pronounces absolution. The officiant then dismisses the penitent, with the traditional request for the penitent's prayers (pp. 447–48).

Form Two is rather more innovative. It draws freely from the Byzantine form of confession, includes the use of Scripture, which parallels the new Roman rite, and explicitly enjoins the ancient tradition of laying hands on the penitent with the absolution.[12] The priest and penitent pray together a portion of Psalm 51, and the penitent asks for and receives the priest's prayer for a good confession. The priest then offers words from the Scripture, with the "Comfortable Words" printed as a model, and bids the penitent's confession. The confession is prefaced with words that incorporate rich biblical imagery and is concluded with a statement of sorrow and repentance. The priest offers "words of comfort and counsel" and then asks the penitent if she or he will turn again to Christ and forgive those who have sinned against her or him. The priest prays that God will receive the confession, lays on hands, and pronounces one of the two absolutions mentioned above. The dismissal of the penitent again draws upon scriptural imagery, and the penitent responds, "Thanks be to God" (pp. 449–51).

The typically Anglican pastoral emphasis is evident throughout both rites, as is their historical continuity with the practice of the Christian Church, both East and West. The rites assure the penitent sinner that God not only forgives the sins of those who repent, in general, but that his or her particular sins are, through the ministry of the Church, authoritatively forgiven and put away. The penitent leaves the place of confession reconciled to God and the Body of Christ. It is also a reformed rite, though, in that confession is not obligatory and not, in any sense, a judicial proceeding. The presumption is apparently made that God, "unto whom all hearts are open, all desires known and from whom no secrets are hid," knows the sincerity of the penitent's contrition and will make the absolution fruitful according to his grace.

The Church trusts, in this action, that God who has promised to forgive sins will keep his promise in ways that surpass human understanding. Precisely how this occurs, the Church leaves up to God. One might say that, in this matter, the position of the *BCP* 1979 is analogous to the classical Anglican position on the "real presence" of Christ in the Eucharist. The Church asserts it in faith, according to God's promises, and leaves God to fulfill them. There is no attempt to go beyond what we can affirm in faith about the mystery of divine activity in the forgiveness of sins through Jesus Christ. The Church has been given the power and authority to proclaim God's pardon, and, in the Reconciliation of the Penitent, the Church does just that through the ministry of those ordained to act on the Church's behalf.

To use our absolution typology, these rites are at once precatory, declaratory, and authoritative. God's pardon is hoped for, proclaimed, and made manifest in the here and now. Being at once eschatological, kerygmatic, and incarnational, the Reconciliation of a Penitent is clearly sacramental. Few contemporary Anglicans are likely to have much trouble regarding it as, indeed, a sacrament, that is, "an outward and visible sign of inward and spiritual grace, given by Christ as [a] sure and certain means by which we receive that grace" (p. 857). It incorporates both the Reformation emphasis that faith is absolutely necessary for the Christian to appropriate God's action in Christ, and the Catholic assertion that the Church has the power to speak God's word concretely and authoritatively. God's action is prior and primary, but the faithful response of the individual is required to make God's grace fruitful. The Prayer Book rites are, thus, classically Anglican in liturgical expression and theology.

The Rite of Penance (1974)

The Second Vatican Council of the Roman Catholic Church,

as part of its sweeping revision of all its liturgies, mandated a new
version of the sacrament of Penance, but it was some time before
this work could be accomplished. The eagerly awaited new *Ordo
Paenitentiae* appeared on December 2, 1973, "by special mandate
of the supreme pontiff." The Latin text came into force immediately, but each national episcopal council was charged with
commissioning and approving a translation into the local ver-
nacular. The approved English-language *Rite of Penance* appeared
in the United States in 1975 and has been used since.[13] The
document is a complete collection of three rites for sacramental
confession, suggested non-sacramental penitential services, co-
pious scriptural readings, extensive directions for use, and interpretative materials.

The Rite of Penance must be seen in its larger context of the
total liturgical reform in the Roman Catholic Church. Certain
principles had already been established, and the rites of penance
are consistent with them. Fr. J. D. Crichton summarizes these
principles as follows:

1) Liturgy is an act of the whole church;
2) There must always be a proclamation of the Word of God;
3) The rites must be visible; and
4) The liturgy must be participatory.[14]

It is further apparent that more is intended than just a revision of
the services of the Church. As the general editor of a three-
volume commentary on the new penitential rites put it,

The new liturgical books call for something far deeper than a
change in ritual: the purpose of the new books is to aid spiritual
renewal in Catholic worship.[15]

Since its publication, the new *Ordo Paenitentiae* has occasioned
extensive commentary throughout the Roman Catholic Church.
That response has been difficult to synthesize for a number of
reasons, among them: the abundance of the material, the shift by
Vatican II from deductive to inductive theology, and the Council
Fathers' concern with accommodating the often differing understandings and practices of the Eastern Churches.[16] Nonetheless,
there is a general consensus that the new rite represents significant
changes, not only in the penitential practices of the Roman Cath-

olic Church, but in its theological understandings as well. Virgil C. Funk, of the Liturgical Conference, writes:

> Several aspects of the sacrament have been consistently misunderstood or de-emphasized throughout its history, and the revised Rite of Penance brings them into focus: viz., the role of Penance in the life of the community, especially in its relation to Baptism and the Eucharist, the nature of Sin, the role and function of the celebrant and the community, the central attention to the act of Reconciliation (as opposed to auricular confession), the necessity of celebration, and the options available in the revised Rite.[17]

The Rite of Penance begins with an extensive Introduction, which sets the new rites in their context and gives general directions for their use. This section parallels that of *The Book of Common Prayer*, but is much broader and more theological. It begins by observing that the Church's ministry of reconciliation is based on Jesus' call to repentance and his reconciling work and death. This work has been given over to the Church and, "since [Pentecost] the Church has never ceased to call men from sin to conversion and by the celebration of penance to show the victory of Christ over sins." This victory is first manifested in Baptism, then in the Sacrifice of the Mass in which the passion of Christ is made present, and in Penance through the power given by Christ to his apostles and their successors to forgive sin.[18] The sacrament of penance must be seen in the context of the Church's very nature; the Church is holy and yet always in need of purification. Thus, it constantly pursues repentance and renewal in a variety of ways. Each Christian's sin disrupts friendship with God and harms the fellowship. Therefore, sin is always corporate, especially in its aspect of injustice.[19]

The sacrament has four parts: contrition, confession, the act of penance, and the absolution. Contrition is the most important act and is *metanoia*, a profound interior change. It is manifested in the confession, the will of the penitent to confess sin and in the minister's "spiritual judgment," by which he retains or remits the sins by the power of the keys. The act of penance, or satisfaction, is a remedy for sin and a help to the renewal of life. Finally, the absolution is an authoritative act of pardon. The sacrament is both necessary and beneficial, and healing in penance is varied. The faithful must confess every grave sin they remember. Frequent confession of venial sins is helpful, as well, in order to help the Christian conform more closely to the pattern of Christ.[20]

The sacrament of Penance is, in one sense, ministered by the whole Church, the priestly people who call men and women to penance by preaching the Word and interceding for them. More especially, the ministers of the rite are a priest or bishop with faculties to absolve, and the penitent whose acts are the most important in the celebration of penance. The rite may be celebrated at any time, but Lent is deemed especially appropriate as the liturgical context of the whole Church's awareness of its corporate need for a life of repentance.[21] Provision is made for the Reconciliation of Several Penitents with Individual Confession and Absolution, and for the Reconciliation of Penitents with General Confession and Absolution. However,

> Individual, integral confession and absolution remain the only ordinary way for the faithful to reconcile themselves with God and the Church, unless physical or moral impossibility excuses from this kind of confession.[22]

The obligation to make a confession once annually remains in force. Thus, the Rite for Reconciliation of Individual Penitents remains normative and is the one we will explore.

The priest and penitent are instructed to begin the celebration with prayer. The priest should then welcome the penitent "with fraternal charity." They make the sign of the cross and the priest urges the penitent to have faith in God, using the words of Scripture, and the penitent makes a confession of sin. The priest offers counsel to aid the penitent in renewal of life and imposes an act of penance or satisfaction appropriate to the penitent and to the gravity of the sin. The penitent manifests contrition and a resolution to begin a new life, using a prayer for God's pardon. The priest pronounces the absolution, of which the words "I absolve you in the name of the Father and of the Son and of the Holy Spirit" are essential. The absolution, which combines precatory, declaratory, and authoritative elements, is accompanied by the sign of the cross or the laying-on of hands. The priest and penitent praise the Lord, and the penitent is dismissed.[23]

Commentators on the new *Rite of Penance* have discerned a remarkable variety of themes in the document and a number of significant changes from the previous penitential rites and theological emphases of the Roman Catholic Church. For extensive elaboration on these themes, the reader is referred to the commentaries themselves; however, for the purposes of this study, we may discern five significant themes. The *Rite* can be understood as including a more holistic approach to the mystery of sin and forgiveness, a more corporate or ecclesial approach, a clearer relation of Penance to the whole liturgical and sacramental life of the Church, a decidedly less legalistic view of the sacrament, and considerably more pastoral concern.

First, from the very beginning of the Introduction, the new *Rite* is concerned with "the mystery of reconciliation in the history of salvation." Reconciliation is not to be seen as an isolated instant in the life of an individual, but rather as part of God's whole creative, redemptive, and sanctifying work in the world.

> Reconciliation, then, is not only the forgiveness of sins. It is also union with Christ and, through him, with the Father. It is the making of a new people with a common destiny and the freedom to go forward to a new way of life.... The word "reconciliation" sums up what Christian life is all about.[24]

We are called to enter into God's work in Christ, which is a redemption and recreation of the whole cosmos. The individual is invited to look beyond his or her own personal sins to the universal love of God, and to the reconciliation of all humanity that that love wills to work in Christ. Fr. Colman Grabert asserts that "the formula of absolution confronts the penitent with the powerful eschatological symbol of a *reconciled world*, the agent of which is God."[25]

Reconciliation is, thus, a matter of the recovery of one's true identity in Christ. Sin is a radical threat to that identity, a flight from responsible selfhood that renders our true identity opaque. Reconciliation opens our eyes to who we really are, deeply related in Christ to God and all others. Part of that identity is a solidarity with the humanity Christ seeks to redeem—sinful and yet created by God—and a membership in the Body of Christ, the first fruits of redeemed humanity.

Thus the penitential avowal of sins to a representative of the community is a death to "self" (a false unrecognizable self) for the sake of a being-with-others, a finding of oneself in others. The act of confession expresses the pentitent's willingness to receive a new self beyond this death, a self constituted by the eschatological symbols of the church, the community of the resurrection.[26]

Because this self and the community are "on the way" and have not yet attained the fullness of redemption, the sacrament of Reconciliation shares in the ambiguity of God's action in time and space:

Just as the entire rite of penance is characterized by the tension between a *hoped-for* reconciliation and an *experienced* alienation, so the historical community lives under the same tension as it moves into the future.[27]

The introduction of eschatology leads us to the second, related theme of the new rites, that is, their corporate or ecclesial character. The revisers seem to be very concerned that Reconciliation not be privatized as a ritual that concerns only the individual. Reconciliation is a primary act of the Church and a statement of its very being. Thus, Reconciliation is a sacramental manifestation of the Church, as, indeed, the Church is a sacramental manifestation of the redemptive work of Christ. The priest and penitent "must see themselves as the community of believers, in this case a community of only two gathered in the name of Jesus."[28] This perspective is helpful not only in relating the penitent to the Church, but in seeing sin in all of its corporate and social aspects. All Christians are reminded of their failure to enter fully into the healin g of this broken world according to the call of Christ.

This insight is based on the best contemporary sacramental theology, which sees the Church itself as the primary sacrament of Jesus in the world. No theologian has spoken more insightfully or powerfully to this point than Karl Rahner, whose scholarship and piety loom large in any discussion of post-conciliar Roman Catholicism. He points out that sin is a disruption in the sinner's effective membership in the Body of Christ, and thus reconciliation through the Church is also reconciliation with the Church.

What happens here in the sacrament of penance is an actualization of the Church's own essence. She is manifested in the penitent himself (who co-operates in her liturgy), as the penitent Church of sinners ever bathing the feet of Christ with her tears and hearing his word, "Neither will I condemn thee." ... It is a vital expression of the Church's essence, as bearer of God's grace-giving words, which she addresses here to the individual and so effectually fulfills her own nature as the abiding society of God's mercy in the world. In the common action of the priest as the authorized spokesman of the Church, and of the penitent human being, the fundamental nature of the Church herself is manifested.[29]

Third, the Church's sacramental nature is particularly manifested in the sacraments in general, and especially in the great Gospel sacraments of Baptism and Eucharist. The new *Rite of Penance* is much more clearly related to those two sacraments. Many commentators recognize that Reconciliation is, as is so often said in the East, a kind of Second Baptism. Further, it is also recognized that the Holy Eucharist is the primary sacrament of ordinary reconciliation of Christians:

> ... The sacrament of penance is a renewal of the baptismal gift of the Spirit, a continuation and extension of the grace of baptism.... The eucharist affirms and celebrates reconciliation [and] is the continuation of Christ's ministry in which he shared table with sinners and outcasts....[30]

An integral part of Roman Catholic liturgical theology and practice since Vatican II has been the recovery of the primary importance of the Word of God. It is, therefore, not surprising that *The Rite of Penance* includes much scriptural material and calls on priest and penitent alike to meditate on, and assimilate, the Word of reconciliation in the Gospel.

Fourth, the recovery of biblical theology has resulted in a much richer understanding of sin than was previously expressed in the Tridentine rite and its typical administration. Commentators agree that the Church *intends* a move away from legalism. Whether this actually happens, of course, will depend on how the rite is administered. One way of looking at the new direction is that it is a shift from an emphasis on sin to an emphasis on sinfulness. That is, in accord with much Protestant theology, sin resides more in the human condition than in particular violations of law. As Fr. Crichton puts it, "Sin ... is a breaking of a loving union with

God, which comes to a great deal more than the infringement of a legal code."[31] The *Rite* takes sin seriously, perhaps more seriously than before, but calls the penitent to look at the whole course and direction of his or her life.

> So long as a morality of law was given primary attention, it was possible to be content with the question, "What have I done?" As the focus shifts to love and justice, the question becomes, "What kind of person am I?"[32]

Administration of Reconciliation should, then, focus more on the underlying disease (sin) than on symptoms (sins), and thus become a more therapeutic and less judicial affair. Above all, it is a celebration of God's mercy and should direct one's attention ultimately to the love of God by which we are forgiven and reconciled.[33]

Finally, it should be obvious that such a rite will call for an intensely pastoral approach in its celebration. No longer is the priest seen as a judge, but much more as a pastor whose "spiritual judgment" is akin to the "discernment of spirits," an ability to "read the soul of the penitent."[34] The pastoral concern is everywhere in the rites and in the instructions for their administration. Priests must choose from a variety of options with an eye toward what will be most helpful to the individual penitent. Local priests and bishops are given significant discretion in ordering and adapting the rites to local circumstances. Even the physical arrangements are intended to make it possible for the confession to be heard face-to-face, in a situation more like a physician's consulting room or a counsellor's study than the dock in a courtroom. It seems fair to say that, as it is in *The Book of Common Prayer*, *The Rite of Penance* in the Roman Catholic Church is now clearly a "pastoral office."

The Lutheran Book of Worship (1978)

In a remarkable stroke of Providence, the day I went to Trinity Lutheran Seminary in Columbus, Ohio, to pursue my research, I found the following note on the door of the chapel:

"Individual Confession and Absolution today in the Shalom Room, 1:00–1:45 p.m., 10:00–11:00 p.m." Upon examination, I found the Shalom Room to be a small side chapel, admirably— and I suspect intentionally—suited for the administration of the rite of Reconciliation. Thus, in the third major "liturgical" church in the West, this pastoral office is also now practiced.

We may recall, from our historical survey, that Luther sought to reform confession, but not to abolish it. His writings give ample evidence of the esteem in which he held the practice, if rightly understood. However, in Lutheran countries as in England, the practice gradually declined and virtually disappeared. Also as in England there was a revival in the mid-nineteenth century. Two notable evangelical German pastors, Christoph Blumhardt and Wilhelm Loehe, revived confession among their parishioners in 1843, although a more general renewal of the practice waited for nearly a century.[35] Dietrich Bonhoeffer, for example, wrote enthusiastically of the great grace of making a confession to a fellow Christian. He believed that such fraternal confession helped the believer break through pride, self-deception, and iso- lation, and that in the brother one meets the whole church to whom one confesses one's sin and from whom one receives the assurance of divine forgiveness.

> Christ became our Brother in order to help us. Through him our brother has become Christ for us in the power and authority of the commission Christ has given to him.... So, in the Christian com- munity, when the call to brotherly confession and forgiveness goes forth it is a call to the great grace of God in the Church.[36]

Since, in Bonhoeffer's view, any Christian with appropriate sen- sitivity can hear a confession, there is yet some distance from the Roman Catholic or Anglican priest-administered sacrament.

An important mid-twentieth-century source for the revival of formal confession in the Lutheran Churches is Herbert Girgen- sohn's *Teaching Luther's Catechism*.[37] In the second volume, which deals with Baptism, Confession, and the Lord's Supper, Girgen- sohn comments at length on Luther's suggestions for confession contained in the *Small Catechism* (see Appendix A). In expressing his hope for a revival of confession in the evangelical church,

Girgensohn states that the power of the keys means that sins are indeed forgiven. Private confession makes forgiveness concrete when the penitent believes in divine mercy and when Jesus himself is behind the Church's action in pronouncing absolution.

> The invisible transaction that occurs between God and man in the secret confession of the heart takes on a tangible form in individual confession, acquires a reality in this human, earthly life which produces real effects.[38]

Girgensohn emphasizes that evangelical confession is voluntary and may be made to any Christian. He notes, however, that the pastor is one whose office obligates him to receive confessions when asked. The validity of the absolution depends solely upon the Word proclaimed in obedience to Christ's command, but the pastor's absolution is valid and efficacious. Whoever serves as confessor must keep the seal of the confessional absolute. The form can be rather free, but the absolution should be authoritative. it is important that confessants affirm their faith that the confessor's absolution is God's. The laying-on of hands is not required, but it does strengthen the healing power of forgiveness.[39] Girgensohn concludes his discussion with these powerful words:

> The introduction of the practice of confession in a congregation must mean that the gospel in its saving power and greatness is again being offered, heard, and received in faith, and that this then produces a proper evangelical understanding of confession. It means further that people have come again to see in the church the possibility of unloading their burdens. This naturally is a primary responsibility of the ministry. The ministry should become the place in the midst of this harried world where somebody is willing to listen and to deal with the distressing realities of life and then in the power and authority of Jesus Christ lead people to the liberating word of absolution.[40]

As the Inter-Lutheran Commission on Worship began to propose revised services, some controversy ensued over the proper placement of penitential material in the service of Holy Communion. No fully satisfactory placement was found. Walter Bouman, commenting on the problem, asserted that the basic confession of sins is baptismal and that the Eucharist pre-supposes baptism and the baptismal confession. He went on to assert that "truly pastoral care for one another in order to enable us continually to reconstitute the eucharistic community requires the restoration—where necessary—of all the forms of confession."[41] Thus, when *The Lutheran Book of Worship* (*LBW*) was published in 1978, it included an order of Individual Confession and Forgiveness, compiled by none other than Walter Bouman.

The order is remarkably similar to that in Luther's *Short Catechism*, which can be presumed to have provided the model. The pastor greets the penitent, ascertaining that the latter is ready to confess. Then, together, they recite several verses of Psalm 51. The pastor bids the confession, and the penitent, with virtually no preface, makes it. Following, "the pastor may then engage the penitent in pastoral conversation, offering admonition and comfort from the Holy Scriptures." Then both say more verses from Psalm 51 and the following exchange ensues, the pastor standing and facing the penitent:

> PASTOR: Do you believe that the word of forgiveness I speak to you comes from God himself?
> PENITENT: Yes, I believe.
> [The pastor lays both hands on the head of the penitent.]
> PASTOR: God is merciful and blesses you. By the command of our Lord Jesus Christ, I, a called and ordained servant of the Word, forgive you all your sins in the name of the Father, and of the Son, and of the Holy Spirit.
> PENITENT: Amen.

Pastor and penitent may pray together, using the words of Psalm 103:8-13, the pastor dismisses the penitent, and they may exchange the peace.[42]

In a section of further instructions, it is suggested that regular times be set aside for the hearing of confessions. The service may be used during counselling sessions, but the pastor should provide a transition from counselling to confession. Individual confession is a helpful, but not required, preparation for receiving Holy Communion. The rubrics go on to state:

> It is inappropriate for anyone not ordained to serve as a confessor. Though this service is done in private, it is a part of the exercise of

the public ministry of the Church and is, therefore, the province of those called and ordained as pastors.

The confidentiality of the confession is absolute, and care should be taken that no one overhears or disturbs the penitent. The penitent kneels, and the pastor may sit in a chair or kneel with the penitent. If penitents are uncomfortable with the form, they should be encouraged to use their own words; the pastor, too, is free to modify the form as circumstances suggest.[43]

In a manual to accompany the *LBW*, commentary on the form of confession is included in the section on the baptismal rites and its use is recommended for "one with a troubled conscience who seeks the consolation of the church." The authors add the long-standing maxim that regular confessors should be under the discipline of regular confession themselves. The tone to be set is pastoral and serious. It is recommended that confessions be heard at the altar rail.

> When the penitent arrives at the appointed place, the pastor greets the penitent. The greeting may be informal but it must be restrained. It is not a time for pleasantries. The pastor may speak to the penitent concerning individual confession, emphasizing the gravity of sin or the need to accept responsibility for sin and its consequences, but the pastor should direct the penitent firmly to the unfailing mercy and grace of God to all who repent and turn to him.[44]

The pastor is finally urged to use Scripture at any point in the rite. There is no suggestion, however, of any act of penance or satisfaction following the absolution. In theology, tone, and sources, while demonstrably part of the Western penitential tradition, this is a thoroughly Lutheran rite.

We have seen, in our examination of the rites of penance and reconciliation in the Episcopal, Roman Catholic, and American Lutheran Churches, a remarkable similarity of form and content (see Appendix B). This testifies to the ecumenical context mentioned at the outset. At the same time, each rite has the flavor of its own particular tradition, showing, perhaps, that one may be ecumenical without losing one's identity.

Reconciliation in Other Churches

Let us take a brief look at the status of Reconciliation in other churches, beginning with the rich penitential tradition of Eastern Orthodoxy. This is a highly pluriform tradition, yet one rooted in the work of the great Greek Fathers of the Church. There is a complex of rites, either public or private, that vary somewhat with each national Church and are called Repentance, Penance, or Confession, and often, with clear echoes of the Fathers, Second Baptism. The private form is a confidential conference with a priest. The rite is often related to the Divine Office, a continuation of the monastic tradition, still strong in Orthodoxy. Confessions are heard in a convenient part of the Church, with priest and penitent standing, usually before a Book of the Gospels or an icon of the Saviour. The priest acts not as a judge, but as a witness, as a physician, as one who speaks for and prays with the penitent. When the confession has been made, the priest places his stole on the penitent's head, lays hands, and pronounces an absolution that may be either precatory or authoritative. The priest may impose a penance, but it is not required. There is no strict rule as to frequency, but where the reception of communion is infrequent, as it often is in Orthodoxy, it is preceded by a confession.[45]

While Christians of the Reformed and Free Church traditions do not seem to be beating on the confessional door, there is some indication that the idea of at least quasi-sacramental reconciliation is not as abhorrent as it used to be. A survey of literature by Protestants shows some directions for the future. We might expect to find an increased appreciation for such reconciliation precisely where Protestants are re-appropriating the more traditionally "catholic" concerns for ecclesiology, ordained ministry, the sacraments, and spiritual direction. These linkages are clear from all of the foregoing.

The great classic in the field is by Max Thurian, a French Reformed pastor and brother of the famous Protestant (now ecumenical) monastic community at Taizé.[46] After a careful survey of Calvin and the other great reformers, he concludes that all signs of a sacrament, in the Reformed sense, are present in the act of absolution:

(1) a particular, concrete and visible character;
(2) divine institution, as the risen Christ explicitly mentions is a part of the whole ministry of the Church;
(3) it is related to the unique sacrifice of Christ on the Cross; and
(4) it is efficacious, a sign that God grants by grace forgiveness of sins and eternal life.[47]

Further, there is great spiritual profit in the sacrament, as it makes the Word concrete for the believer.

> The sacrament of absolution therefore effectually confers what it signifies. God's word announcing the promise of mercy made by Jesus Christ must be made concrete in the sign of absolution; and the believer must realize that the remission of sins is not only a hope but an actual fact to which he can hold fast with all his faith.[48]

For Thurian, the revival of confession in Protestantism is linked with a deepened appreciation for the Church as the Body of Christ and the believer's membership in the communion of the saints. This emphasis on the corporate aspect of Christian identity is meant as an antidote to Protestant individualism. Thurian also locates the practice of confession in a movement toward a Protestant recovery of spiritual direction and guidance. Thus, it must be voluntary and fairly informal, with the penitent's need determining the circumstances and form. Pastor Thurian does, however, seem to regard the ordained minister as the normative confessor. To put flesh on his arguments, he offers a suggested means of self-examination and a form for the confession. The latter is based on Roman Catholic practice of the time (1953), with adaptations appropriate to Reformed sensibilities. It concludes with this absolution:

> The Lord breathed on his disciples and said unto them, Receive ye the Holy Ghost: Whose soever sins ye remit, they are remitted unto them; and whose soever sins ye retain, they are retained. [The confessor may lay his hands on the penitent.] May our Lord Jesus Christ absolve thee; and I by his authority do absolve thee from every bond of sin. Thus do I grant theee absolution from thy sins, in the name of the Father, and of the Son, and of the Holy Ghost. Amen.[49]

Calvin might approve, but one is not quite sure latterday Calvinists would. Nonetheless, Thurian's work is probably the most impor-

tant work by a Reformed writer on the subject and will be a major
source for any Protestant revival of Reconciliation.

For several decades, in America at least, pastoral ministry has
been heavily related to psychotherapy through the pastoral counselling movement. It has been claimed, with some justice, that this
represents an evolution of the Reformed tradition of pastoral care
through visitation and catechetical conversation. It is, therefore,
not surprising to find an appreciation of the possibilites of confession arising from this quarter. In the work of George William
Bowman, a Baptist hospital chaplain and counsellor, this is exactly
the case.[50] Bowman is especially interested in the possibilities of a
"Protestant functional confession" that may help relieve guilt and
which, when freed from legalism and mechanical administration,
has a legitimate place in Protestantism's ministry to souls.

According to Bowman, the aims of confession are focalization
[sic] of sin, articulation of sinful attitudes and acts, direction
toward relief of guilt, assurance of God's forgiveness, discovery of
appropriate restitution, and the realization of absolution. The
latter is especially problematic and will take much effort on the
part of the confessor:

> No matter how strongly the confessor feels that God has forgiven
> the sinner with whom he has been working, this does not avail the
> confessant. What is of utmost importance is that the confessant feel
> and know that he is forgiven by God. To know in oneself that he has
> been forgiven is realized absolution.[51]

This psychological and rather subjective approach lacks any ecclesial dimension and by-passes the question of whether or not one
must be ordained to perform this ministry; it also suggests no rites
or forms. Nonetheless, it is an important effort to relate Reconciliation to the extensive literature on pastoral care.

Two recent works can conclude this survey. In his massive
Pastoral Theology, Thomas Oden calls for the revival of the "classical
pastoral tradition" of the past two thousand years. His view of
ministry is fully sacramental, and he quotes at length from Fathers
and Doctors of the Catholic Church and the Reformers, as well.
He wants to restore to the ordained minister a primary responsibility for "the care of souls," and this includes allusions to what
might be taken as some form of "hearing confessions." He rather

clearly rejects auricular confession in its mediaeval form, however, in favor of what he sees as the apostolic pattern of house-to-house visitation. The latter includes rather heavy listening as the means to satisfy the legitimate need of "the human spirit to unburden itself in the presence of a trusted companion who could mediate the forgiveness of God amid human sin."[52]

Finally, Richard Foster, a Quaker, devotes a chapter of his very influential book on Christian spiritual disciplines to "The Discipline of Confession." He believes that the followers of Jesus Christ have been given the authority to hear the confessions of their brothers and sisters and to forgive in his name. Since all believers are priests of God, they share in Christ's priesthood by standing in his stead to make God's presence and forgiveness real to us. For Foster, a "stylized form" of confession has advantages as a "Reality Therapy of the best sort," enabling us to own responsibility for our sins. Further, the word of forgiveness is expected and given in the absolution, and we are given a means to consider the seriousness of our sins.[53]

Foster's work is rooted in the consistent tradition, from Cassian to the Pietists, of mutual confession to one another by Christians. Although he asserts that all Christians may hear confession, not all are gifted with sufficient empathy and understanding to be helpful. Again, we see a part of the whole tradition being brought to our attention, although a full sacramental ministry of Reconciliation is only potentially present. That Protestants are interested in this tradition at all represents a significant recovery of a promising ministry. We can conclude with a vigorous Amen to Foster's call:

> The Discipline of confession brings an end to pretense. God is calling into being a church that can openly confess its frail humanity and know the forgiving and empowering graces of Christ. Honesty leads to confession, and confession leads to change. May God give grace to the church once again to recover the Discipline of confession.[54]

The Theology of Reconciliation: Toward an Ecumenical Synthesis

We will now attempt to draw together a working theology of Reconciliation incorporating insights and understandings emerging from a variety of traditions. In the late twentieth century, this is easier to do than it has been for many centuries of the Christian experience. There is a remarkable convergence of thought on this subject in the Anglican, Roman Catholic, Lutheran, and even the Reformed, traditions. Thus, while every item we propose will not be fully acceptable as stated to all Christians in these traditions, I dare to believe that its broad contours would be generally embraced by most. We will be working, as is so often the case in Christian theology, by asserting polar tensions in a kind of dialectic, always trying to prefer the both/and to the either/or.

I can illustrate this dialectical approach best by using a cogent observation of Ladislas Orsy. In *The Evolving Church and the Sacrament of Penance*, he notes that the Mediterranean (or Patristic) penitential system was based on a strong consciousness of the unity of the Christian community. It was thus concerned primarily with reconciliation to the community. On the other hand, the Irish system was based on the understanding that sin was a break in the relationship with God, and, therefore, penance was highly individualized. These emphases came into conflict, and the conflict was, in Orsy's view, resolved mostly in favor of the Irish system by Trent.[55] I do not think this conflict inevitable and would suggest that both elements need to be held in tension in any adequate theology of Reconciliation.

If Reconciliation is seen primarily as the individual's effort to "square things" with God in a private conversation between priest and penitent, then we get what Kenneth Ross describes as "the modern atomized and individualistic absolution" for which there is no warrant in the New Testament.[56] On the other hand, an excessive emphasis on the community can lead to a purely horizontal approach to the rite, an approach that is easily formalized and trivialized. We have heard too much facile talk about "community" in the Church in the last two decades; the mystery of divine forgiveness does not operate only at the human level. Reconciliation must be understood as *both* with God and with the Church. Put another way, it is a matter of both *conversion* and *community*.

Another tension which we must hold as we consider the theology of Reconciliation is the classical one between God's action and human response to that action. This is the very ancient dialectic of faith and works, of grace and moral effort. Again, it is a matter of both/and. Without venturing too far into that tangled thicket, let us assert that God's forgiveness and reconciliation of sinners is primary. God's action is all; God's grace is sufficient. And yet, for that grace to be fruitful in the lives of Christians, they must respond to it with faith and repentance. Perhaps the most helpful notion is that characteristically Eastern theme of *synergy*, a cooperation of human spirit and Holy Spirit. We shall see this played out, not only in the aforementioned themes of conversion and community, but also in our third concern, that is, *sacrament*. It is under these three headings that we shall attempt our "ecumenical synthesis" of the theology of Reconciliation.

When we speak of *conversion* in the late-twentieth-century American context, we must quickly make clear what we do *not* mean. Conversion is not *simply* a once-and-for-all moment of turning to God in Christ, although such a moment may be deeply significant for many people. Conversion, in the classical sense we use here, is a life-long process by which we grow in the knowledge and love of God, in the ability to live faithfully, and to become more and more the person God made us and calls us to be. Conversion is an important word catholic Christians must reclaim from its Pietist corruption. As Urban T. Holmes puts it,

> Grace is the presence of God. His presence is God's free gift of himself to us. Conversion as the coming to awareness of God's solicitation to us is a growth in grace. Day by day, we discover God in our lives, calling us into being more than we are already. The invitation is to live in the Kingdom.[57]

Sin is not so much a matter of certain acts that violate an external law, but rather a matter of the directions of our lives and, at bottom, a question of our personal identity.

> In the most radical sense, what makes human beings sinners are not wicked deeds; the deeds are merely manifestations of the existential condition of hostility and helplessness.[58]

Therefore, conversion, in which the rite of Reconciliation can play such an important part, strikes at the root causes of our sinful acts by addressing our sinful self. It is an admission of my responsibility to be the person God calls me to be. It is a turning away from evil and toward God, both in interior direction and exterior behavior, a death to self that I might live in Christ. Holmes follows Bernard Longergan and describes conversion as being religious, intellectual, and moral all at once.[59] This schema is helpful and consistent with much contemporary thinking on Reconciliation.

The religious dimension of conversion involves a "falling in love with God." Indeed, this metaphor embraces both the momentary and life-long aspects of conversion. When we fall in love with a human being, we may be aware of a particular moment when "it happened," but we are also aware that living out the love is a matter of a lifetime. In conversion, we come to be aware of how much God loves us and how much we want to love God, although we fall desperately short of the love that would fulfill our humanity.

> The Christian sense of sin, then, involves a person, and specifically a person who loves us. Sin is essentially a religious concept. The better we understand God and his love for us, the better we will understand sin and transgression.... Sin will then be seen as a disfigurement of love. It will be seen as the "No" with which we can answer God's invitation to live with him in love, and as a decision to live without the life this love brings.[60]

We experience our sinfulness at the religious level as alienation, estrangement from our true selves and from the source of our life. We are, as it were, out of love. Like the Prodigal, we have wandered far in a land that is waste and desire to return to where we find love. As Monika Hellwig puts its:

> The deep human need to which the sacrament is addressed is the need to return to the Father's house from exile, to come home to one's true place, to find liberation from fear, boredom and frustration, to find one's authentic existence behind the many masks of unreality, to find peace from restlessness, anxiety and discontent, to find a bottomless inner peace with God, with other people and all fellow-creatures, with one's own dependency and limitations and with the uncertainty of the future and the certainty of death.[61]

Sacramental reconciliation is, then, a call to conversion at the religious level, an invitation to come home and embrace the Father who stands at the head of the lane waiting for us in love.

At the intellectual level, conversion is a matter of perception, of *seeing* the world as it is, of seeing ourselves as we are, sinful and yet redeemed in Christ. It is a matter of discernment and insight, of being "de-programmed" from the secular, reductionist, and ego-centric way of thinking characteristic of our culture. We learn to see ourselves as children of God, to see others as brothers and sisters, and to see the world as the Kingdom God is bringing about and would call us to join.

> The challenge of conversion is not the challenge of accepting Jesus' ethical teaching, but the more basic challenge of *recognizing God at work in the world*, establishing a kingdom (or "reign") which is surprising, unexpected and even scandalous.... "Repent!" means to *recognize* in Jesus of Nazareth the ultimate manifestation of God's sovereign action in the world.[62]

This same theme is expressed in *The Book of Common Prayer*. At Baptism, the officiant prays that God will give the baptized "an inquiring and discerning heart, the courage to will and to persevere, a spirit to know and to love you, and the gift of joy and wonder in all your works" (p. 308). At the Holy Eucharist, in Eucharistic Prayer C, the celebrant prays, "Open our eyes to see your hand at work in the world about us" (p. 372). The very concreteness of sacramental reconciliation works at our intellectual conversion by directing our attention both to our own sinfulness and to the presence of God in our broken lives.

The discussion of religious and intellectual conversion is a necessary prologue to any consideration of its moral aspect. We cannot truly act morally in the world without the love of God in our hearts and our eyes open. Efforts at moral conversion alone leads to moralism, to self-righteousness, to frustration, and to legalism. As we are converted, as we repent, we will act more faithfully, more morally, of course, but these external acts flow from an interior turning. Moral conversion is an effort to respond to the call of John the Baptist to "bear fruit that befits repentance" (Matthew 3:8 and parallels). Such moral conversion is a cooperation with the leading of the Holy Spirit. As Monika Hellwig observes, acts of penitence:

> can only fulfill the function of free, creaturely participation in that

transformation of being, vision, relationships and actions knowing
that the transformation is a free gift of grace and therefore a gift to
be received in our freedom.[63]

Sacramental reconciliation enables us to use more faithfully that
creaturely freedom that is God's gift to us, as we are empowered by
the Spirit.

Tad Guzie and John McIlhon have described sacramental
confession as "a peak moment in a total process of conversion."[64]
The process, in its religious, intellectual, and moral dimensions, is
a divinely assisted effort to recover our truest identity and to live
that identity out by grace.

> Reconciliation in the New Testament does not consist in plea-
> bargaining with God. Nor does it have anything to do with amass-
> ing virtue so that God will be forced, in justice, to bestow grace and
> salvation. If the radical meaning of repentance is "recognition and
> response," then the meaning of reconciliation is *obedience* and *sur-
> render*. Being obedient to the word of the Gospel does not mean the
> perfect fulfilling of laws, regulations and prescriptions. It means,
> instead, letting go, giving up our pretentious claims to goodness
> and holiness, surrendering to the power of God's love that burns
> even our virtues away.[65]

The call to a renewed sense of *community* in Reconciliation
must strike Anglican ears with a particular urgency. In recent
history, it has been a highly individual and private practice, with
no overt and explicit relationship to the other rites and sacraments
of the Church. For many Anglicans, it seems idiosyncratic and
arcane, "all right, if you need that sort of thing." Even for regular
penitents, it would have been hard to see anything but a fairly
private transaction with one's confessor or spiritual father. John
Gunstone, writing in 1966, was surely right when he said,

> We need a fuller and more flexible liturgy of penance, a liturgy
> which demonstrates that reconciliation with God is also reconcilia-
> tion with the Church, and which teaches that the individual can
> only be truly penitent in as much as he has surrendered himself to
> the corporality of God's people. For to the extent that we grow aware
> of what the Church is, of what we are in the Church, and of how the
> Church's sacramental life is the expression of her inner reality—to
> that extent will the sacrament of penance take on its true meaning.
> It will no longer remain the place where a few devout souls "confess
> their sins"; it will become the moment when the communal work of
> Christ in his Church either begins anew or grows to fuller stature.[68]

Whether The Reconciliation of a Penitent in the 1979 *Book of Common Prayer* will accomplish this worthy end, only time will tell. The present theological climate, however, is a supportive atmosphere for such a hope.

We can see this concern for what Roman Catholic theologians call the *ecclesial* aspect of Reconciliation, not only throughout *The Rite of Penance*, but in the very placement of such a rite in *The Book of Common Prayer* and *The Lutheran Book of Worship*. Clearly, these latter churches wish their members to understand Reconciliation to be fully a part of the "sacraments, rites and ceremonies" of the Church. The revised rites in all churches seek to recover a vital sense of the Church as the Body of Christ and of all worship as essentially corporate. This is certainly a recovery of the New Testament and Patristic understanding of the Church.

For this view to take adequate root, however, it must be accompanied not just by rhetoric, but by an embodied commitment to discipline and prayer within the Church. Throughout the Western Church, there is a developing renewal of thinking on Baptism and realization that this entails one's incorporation into a community that seeks to live out a faithful obedience to Christ. The expression of Baptism is the ministry of all the Church and all its members.[67] For this ministry, all must be accountable to one another. True mutual ministry, or total ministry, will not be possible without a deep revival of a sense of commitment to one another, which has been historically expressed as ecclesiastical discipline. I am not suggesting, of course, that we measure the Church's vitality by the number of excommunications, nor by the number of anything! Rather, we must make clear that Baptism into the Church of Jesus Christ means the acceptance of a way of life that is total and distinctive. Through sacramental reconciliation, Christians are helped to face the demands of that life and their failures to accept them, not in devastating judgment but in sustaining mercy.

The other side to a revival of discipline is intercession. Modern Christians need to know that their sisters and brothers not only expect great things from them but are deeply involved in their struggles. This means a profound corporate prayer for all members of the Body, and especially for sinners—but of course that means all Christians. In our prayer for one another we recognize our solidarity both in sin and grace. By the Spirit, we are empowered to fall and rise again, with more than a little help from our friends in the Lord. As Godfrey Diekmann observes:

> The traditional image of the church as a matron with outstretched arms is realized in action in the sacrament of reconciliation when the whole Christian assembly prays for its sinful members, trusting in God's promise of mercy, and thus praying in an "infallible" way.[68]

Virtually all contemporary commentators locate Reconciliation as part of the Church's pastoral ministry to her members. Broadly speaking, we can understand pastoral ministry to be the effort to mediate divine healing so that Christians can be more faithful and effective members of the Body. It is the effort to make the healing power of Christ present in concrete and specific ways in the lives of particular persons. The early Church's practice of discipline was intended to restore the penitent, as well as to preserve the integrity of the Church. Monika Hellwig notes a basic Patristic consensus that "binding and loosing" was the responsibility of the Church, exercised by presbyters and bishops. It assumed organic connections between membership in the Church and entrance into the Kingdom, the power of the keys and the implementation of the mercy of God, personal conversion and the reconciling response of the Church.[69] That reconciling response, however, is not confined to those already members in the Church; it extends to the whole world which is, in principle, reconciled to God in Christ.

Reconciliation is not just a pastoral function, it is also prophetic. A proper ecclesiology understands the Church as God's particular agent for the establishment of the Kingdom in time and space. The Church is not just an institution, but a servant; solidarity among its members must mean solidarity with all humankind, and especially with those who suffer. This truth is all too often evaded by the comfortable and affluent Christians of the First World, but today's Church is blessed with prophets who continually recall us to it. The model for the Church's ministry is the ministry of Jesus the Suffering Servant in his profound identification with the sick, the bereaved, the outcast, and the oppressed. As J. D. Crichton puts it, Reconciliation must be "an effort to live out the implications of Baptism in which we were first made like Christ and received our calling to suffer with him that we may rise to new life with him."[70]

The practice of Reconciliation must be linked to a genuine commitment to social justice, by individual Christians and the Church as a whole. As Monika Hellwig observes, "The goal is a deep conversion of hearts expressing itself gently and spontaneously in a conversion of life and therefore of the structures of society."[71] What we need, through the ministry of Reconciliation, is a universalization of the prayer for a newly married couple:

> Make their life together a sign of Christ's love to this sinful and broken world, that unity may overcome estrangement, forgiveness heal guilt, and joy conquer despair (*BCP*, p. 429).

To speak of any action by the Church as a sign to the world is, of course, to speak a language of *sacrament*. We owe a tremendous debt to those theologians of all traditions who have led us away from the view of the sacraments as "transactions" to a deeper, richer, and more classical view. In this, we understand Jesus as the primal sacrament of God's presence in the world, and the Church as the *ur-sacrament* of Christ. This linkage of incarnation and sacrament is especially congenial to Anglicanism. A sacrament is an act of the Christian Church that proclaims and manifests the saving love of God in Christ. All sacraments are an *anamnesis* of the love of God to be appropriated in faith.

> The Church is the fundamental, collective, institutional sacrament that by its very existence tells all human beings that they are already saved in Jesus Christ. At the same time she calls all these human beings to lay effective hold on salvation and reconciliation (which we are always being offered) as a reality already existing and, at the same time, as an invitation to the utterly new.[72]

The central sacraments of the Gospel, Baptism and Eucharist, are preeminently sacraments of reconciliation because they proclaim, manifest, and celebrate the reality of divine love. Baptism, the fundamental sacrament of Christian identity, is our entry into the reconciled and reconciling community. Nathan Mitchell eloquently describes how the Eucharist is a proclamation of Jesus' reconciling work:

In his ministry, then, Jesus combined two important items. He joined his proclamation of the Kingdom with the intimacy of table fellowship—i.e. he combined parable in word (preaching) with parable in action (meal). Secondly, Jesus united the intimacy of table fellowship with the joyful news that sins are forgiven. By welcoming sinners at table Jesus was saying, in effect: your sins are forgiven; the kingdom of God is open to you. Through the fellowship of the table, Christians continued to experience Jesus' invitation to faith and forgiveness. Table and Kingdom became signs of a reconciled existence, of a final communion to which all men and women are destined. In the common sharing of bread and cup, Christians experienced the power of God at work in Christ to reconcile the world.[73]

So, too, all the "minor sacraments" are the particular manifestations of the universal sacrament of God's presence. They are important and valuable because we live in the particularity of time, place, and circumstance. They are means we use to profess our faith in the crises and turning points of our lives. They, too, are the means by which the Church makes known the Gospel in power.

Far from being an occasion of private surgery where sins are aborted in secret, reconciliation publicly announces the central paradox of Christian faith: the fact that the words "God," "love," and "sinner" must be put together in the same sentence.[74]

In this context, the question of the appropriate minister of Reconciliation is the same with respect to any sacrament. The appropriate normative minister of Reconciliation is that person who can pronounce absolution with the full weight of sacramental validity, that person who is recognized by the Church as authorized to act on its behalf. In most traditions, this is someone ordained. This is not to say that sacramentality is necessarily absent if a confession is heard and God's forgiveness proclaimed by someone not ordained. That is, I believe, an open question. Laypersons have always been permitted to baptize in emergency, and in many Protestant traditions "lay elders" preside at the Eucharist.

Catholic tradition would hold, however, that the ministry of the ordained *ensures* that what the Church intends is carried out sacramentally. A Christian may, therefore, make a confession directly to God, to a fellow Christian, or to an ordained minister, a presbyter. All are, in some sense, valid sacramentally; but the full assurance that one is acting in accord with the Church and that the absolution one receives does come with the "power of the keys" is to be found in the ministry of the ordained. Pastorally speaking, after all, the assurance of pardon is the principal reason for sacramental reconciliation. The Lutheran rite witnesses to this by requiring the penitent to affirm the belief that the pastor's absolution comes from God.

Although the term is not common, we can certainly describe the minister of Reconciliation as the "celebrant" or, in the increasingly common usage, the "president," the one who convenes the congregation of two to celebrate the Church's liturgy. And this is what all the sacraments do. They celebrate the loving presence of the Lord Jesus in human life. We have come a long way in our spiritual discernment when we can "celebrate penance/reconciliation," taking the reality of sin seriously, but taking even more seriously the mercy of God. Let us conclude this survey with two remarkably consistent statements on this theme, one Roman Catholic and one Anglican. Frs. Guzie and McIlhon remind us:

> We do not go to confession to "get" forgiveness. We go there to celebrate it. The experience of grace is already there, the love of God is already there. Confession is not itself the new beginning. The new beginning has begun before we come to the sacrament and before absolution is given. Sacramental confession celebrates something that has already begun.[75]

Robert Farrar Capon, that delightful theological gadfly of the Episcopal Church, ends his discussion of Penance as a prime illustration of the non-transactional essence of the sacraments in this way:

> Once you get rid of the transactional emphasis, Penance takes on a new meaning. It's not a special piece of business by which you purchase something you couldn't get elsewhere, but a special party at which you celebrate what you have always had, but were lately, perhaps, guilty of neglecting. There are the two of you—priest and penitent, a couple of perpetually forgiven sinners—telling each other, from different points of view, incredible old stories about what a friend you have in Jesus. Look how many problems that solves. It makes Penance a real sacrament again—a signal instance

new meaning. It's not a special piece of business by which you
purchase something you couldn't get elsewhere, but a special party
at which you celebrate what you have always had, but were lately,
perhaps, guilty of neglecting. There are the two of you—priest and
penitent, a couple of perpetually forgiven sinners—telling each
other, from different points of view, incredible old stories about
what a friend you have in Jesus. Look how many problems that
solves. It makes Penance a real sacrament again—a signal instance
of something that is true everywhere but effectively manifested
here.[76]

When an individual's life of repentance and conversion is
joined to the Church's corporate effort to live out the life of faith as
the Body of Christ given life by the Holy Spirit, holy and yet in
constant need of renewal, and the message of God's forgiving love
is manifested, proclaimed, and celebrated with power—then,
there is the sacrament of Reconciliation.

IV

Pastoral Resources
For Reconciliation

CHRISTIAN life and doctrine often proceed by paradox, by the simultaneous affirmation of two apparent opposites that nonetheless constitute one truth. The sacrament of Reconciliation shares fully in this quality of paradox: we are at once sinners and yet forgiven, God's mercy is sovereign and yet must be received by a person to be fruitful, it is all a matter of grace, and yet we must cooperate. The Gospels often present us with paradoxical images and metaphors that we can only affirm in order to see the whole truth. The call of Jesus is the call to immediate, decisive and whole-hearted decision, and yet conversion-repentance-*metanoia* is a life-long process. "*Be* perfect, as your heavenly Father is perfect," he says, and yet we also must strive to make progress toward perfection, which is always a goal and never fully attained. It is often easier to hear the words of evolution, process, progress than the call to decision, yet both are part of our call.

The sacrament of Reconciliation may, in some caseees, mark one of those decisive moments of turning; it will be a powerful manifestation of the Holy Spirit in time of crisis and *kairos*. Nonetheless, most of the time, it is more likely that sacramental reconciliation will play a role in a lifetime of growth in faithfulness, love, and service. Thus, we need to examine growth and progress in the Christian life, and we could do worse than to recall Ephesians:

> And his gifts were that some should be apostles, some prophets, some evangelists, some pastors and teachers, to equip the saints for the work of ministry, for building up the body of Christ, until we all

attain to the unity of the faith and of the knowledge of the Son of
God, to mature manhood, to the measure of the stature of the
fullness of Christ; so that we may no longer be children, tossed to
and fro and carried about with every wind of doctrine, by the
cunning of men, by their craftiness in deceitful wiles. Rather,
speaking the truth in love, we are to grow up in every way into him
who is the head, into Christ, from whom the whole body, joined
and knit together by every joint with which it is supplied, when each
part is working properly, makes bodily growth and upbuilds itself
in love. (Ephesians 4:11-16)

Our task in this chapter, then, is to consider how men and women
grow to human maturity, to the fullness of their humanity in
Christ.

We will do this by examining resources from three related
disciplines: spiritual direction, developmental psychology, and
faith development. From these fields of study and practice we can
gain insights, theoretical perspectives, concepts, and resources
that will better enable the ministry of reconciliation in the Church.
The first is more obviously part of the Christian tradition and has
been intimately associated with Reconciliation for centuries. The
second and third can provide us with deeper understanding of
the human person, the one who comes to the Church seeking
absolution. It is, after all, a particular person, with a life history
and a unique endowment of gifts and wounds, to whom the
sacrament is addressed. The more we know about what it means to
be human, the more effective we shall be in this ministry. As part of
our survey of the psychological literature of human development,
we shall be especially interested in one form of its reappropriation
by those concerned with religious issues: the growing body of data
and theory about the development of faith. Based on our survey,
we will develop a critical synthesis of various views of psychological, moral, and spiritual development for use by those engaged in
pastoral ministry.

Spiritual Growth and Spiritual Direction

One of the fundamental concerns of Christian ministry from
the earliest days is what the Latin Fathers called *cura animarum*, the

"cure of souls." This has involved many aspects of what we now call pastoral care, but chief among them is the effort to assist Christians in growth toward maturity in Christ, chiefly through prayer. Those undertaking this ministry have been variously called spiritual directors, guides, soul friends, ghostly fathers, spiritual friends, *startsi*, or even gurus. Whatever it is called, the goal is generally the same: to enable fellow Christians to grow in their relationship with God in prayer and to express more fully that relationship in lives lived according to the call of Christ. In this effort, it is assumed, the Christian is assisted by the Holy Spirit as he or she progresses toward greater holiness and perfection.

There is a considerable body of literature about this quest, much of it being recovered and added to in our own day. It tends to have two complementary foci: ascetical theology and spiritual direction. We will look briefly at both. Since it is a vast literature, we will attempt only a survey, concentrating primarily on Anglican sources[1] or within what Martin Thornton calls The English School, the tradition of which *The Book of Common Prayer* is the most notable expression. This school is characterized by:

(1) The affective-speculative synthesis;
(2) a strong pastoral insistence on the unity of the Church militant;
(3) a unique humanism and a unique optimism;
(4) the foundation of Christian life in liturgy, notably the Eucharist and Daily Office;
(5) habitual recollection as more important than formal private prayer at set times according to some method; and
(6) spiritual direction as fundamental to pastoral practice and a source of ascetical theology.[2]

The term "spirituality" has become popular lately and can be misunderstood. Its proper use assumes that human beings are fundamentally spiritual creatures, a unity of mind, body, emotions and will, given life and power by the Holy Spirit. Spirituality is the way men and women live out their full humanity in Christ. As Thornton puts it,

> Spirituality is not pietism but the total practice of every aspect of Christian living. A "spiritual" life is one in which the spirit of God, sought and nurtured in prayer, controls its every minute and every aspect.[3]

In this life, prayer predominates, not as some activity we occasionally stop and "do," but as the very substance of our relationship wtih God, our creator, redeemer, and sustainer. To enable this, the Church has developed ascetical theology as the theory and spiritual direction as the praxis of spirituality.

Thornton describes ascetical theology as a "map" or chart, "against which the position, needs, and capacity of a particular spiritual life can be calculated."[4] Asceticism, in its proper use, comes from a Greek word meaning "discipline" or "training." Ascetical theology is thus, as Leech put it,

> that activity within the Body of Christ which seeks to find out and use the methods, techniques and principles which will aid the growth of the life of prayer. In the process, it will also find out those which hinder this growth.[5]

In a sense, all Christian theology is ascetical theology, as all Christian life is "faith seeking understanding." Nonetheless, asceticl theology is a useful disciplinary focus for making the riches of the Christian tradition in prayer and practice. It is "a mutual working out of ways and means to attain the particular perfection of a unique soul, and it is qualified by a sane and yet real love between two people knit in Christ."[5] It is an activity and ministry of the Christian Church made concrete and specific for the individual. In the Anglican tradition, such guidance is, to use Thornton's term, "empirical," that is, related to the uniqueness of the individual seeking guidance, based on free give and take, in a kind of informed experimentation. The image of the physician is frequently used, and Leech reminds us that the "cure of souls" has the double sense of healing and care. The ultimate source of healing and care is the Holy Spirit, of whom the guide or director is the instrument. As Tilden Edwards cogently observes,

> Being a spiritual friend is being the physician of a wounded soul. And what does a physician do when someone comes in with a bleeding wound? Three things: He or she cleanses the wound, aligns the sundered parts, and gives it rest. That's all. The physician does *not* heal. He or she provides an *environment* for the dominant natural processes of healing to take its course. The physician really is midwife rather than healer.[7]

If obstacles to growth are cleared away, and the Christian is directed to paths and practices that allow the Spirit to work, using the resources of ascetical theology and the practical resources of the relationship with the guide, then, by grace, an individual will make progress toward a deeper life of prayer, expressed in action. The proof of the value of the relationship will be the way the Christian lives out his or her call to full humanity. That more faithful life will consist in the overcoming of sin and a greater freedom in Christ. He or she will be less alienated and more reconciled to self, to neighbor, and to God. Perfection in this life is never reached, but progress is the sign, as well as the result, of a fundamental openness to God. Karl Rahner, the eminent Jesuit theologian, has written:

> We again start with the almost intuitive, unreflective conviction that the Christian ought to *become* holy, that he in some way or other becomes this slowly, that he can become ever *more perfect*, that he is capable of growing in holiness and love of God, and that he moves himself toward a definite goal in his religious and moral life, a goal which is not a simple question of a goal not attained or not yet attained, but a goal towards which he really moves by approaching nearer and nearer to it.[8]

Given this emphasis on the progression of spiritual life, it is not surprising that many ascetical theologians have sought to map out that progress in stages. Throughout the history of Christian tradition such schemes have been many, but the most generally accepted one is the "three ways" first developed by Maximus the Confessor in the seventh century, elaborated as the "triple way" by Bonaventure in the twelfth, and further refined by the great Spanish mystics, Theresa of Avila and John of the Cross in the sixteenth century.[9] According to this schema, the Christian begins the spiritual pilgrimage on the "purgative way," marked by repentance, mortification of the flesh, and a turning away from sin. This leads to the "illuminative way," in which he or she learns more and more of God and His presence becomes more real. Finally, at least for a few, the path culminates in the "unitive way," in which the human soul is one with God in wordless ecstasy. In certain versions of this path, a particular type of prayer is appropriate for each way: discursive meditation (prayer and reflection with words)

for purgation, affective prayer for illumination, and contemplation (or prayer of simplicity, wordless prayer) in union.[10]

There are other views of the progressions of the spiritual life,
and the image of the ladder is often used. All the views tend to
bear some resemblance to the Threefold Way. St. Thomas Aquinas "personalized" the schema and referred to three types of
Christians: beginners, proficients, and the perfect (*incipientes, pro-
ficientes, perfecti*). Kenneth Leech argues that the three paths are
reflected in the Gospel—being the ways of repentance, life in the
Spirit, and perfection—and goes on to say,

> The notion of spiritual progress is an essential element in the
> biblical revelation, for its concern is with the progress of a people,
> progress marked by sin and repentance, by wilderness and exile, by
> conflict and struggle.[11]

Spiritual direction is needed to help the pilgrim determine where
he or she is on the journey, develop appropriate forms of prayer,
interpret spiritual experiences, and modify practice as he or she
moves toward or onto another part of the path. To use Thornton's
word, the Threefold Way is useful as a "map" for spiritual guidance.

Karl Rahner warns against excessive literalism in the use of
this schema, or any schema, in attempting to chart the spiritual
life. He observes that growth in grace is not readily quantifiable,
since grace is not a "thing" to be measured. Nor is there evidence
that such steps always occur in a particular life in a rigid, one-after-
the-other sequence. Rahner argues that we need to know more
about each individual seeker, and especially about that person's
"vital situation," the nature of external circumstances beyond the
person's control, and the individual's life journey and personal
history. In order to do this, we may find a psychology of age
groups and life experience to be "one of the elements required for
a construction of a typical line (or lines) of development necessary
as a neutral substratum for the step-by-step development of the
spiritual life."[12]

To further spiritual progress, discernment and discipline are
needed. In the beginnings of spiritual direction, among the Desert Fathers of the fourth and fifth centuries, discernment, or

diakrisis, was very important, and it has been a consistent theme in ascetical theology since. Perhaps the most noted theorist was Ignatius Loyola, who developed fairly elaborate rules for the "discernment of spirits," and this continues to be an integral part of Jesuit spiritual direction. In the Ignatian model, there are two sets of rules: one set for dealing with temptations and desolations, and the other for distinguishing between God-inspired thoughts and movements and the deceptions of the devil.[13]

Discipline looms large in any consideration of spiritual direction, precisely because progress is generally impossible without effort. An incredible variety of spiritual disciplines have been developed throughout Christian history. They include methods of meditation, rules of life, devotional practices, spiritual reading, physical acts, mortifications of the flesh, and, quite frequently, the regular use of sacramental confession. One such ascetical system, and perhaps the most important for Anglicans, is what Martin Thornton calls the Threefold Rule. This consists of weekly participation in the Eucharist, some form of the Daily Office, and personal devotion, concentrating primarily on scriptural meditation to engender habitual recollection of God's presence. Thornton argues that this is the basic ascetical system of *The Book of Common Prayer* and can be seen in the earliest records of the Christian community (Acts 2:42—apostolic teaching, breaking of bread, the prayers).[14]

In both discernment and discipline, sacramental reconciliation can play an important role. In tracing the history of Reconciliation, John Gunstone argues that, during the Patristic Period, the canonical public form of penance had no real relation to spiritual direction. The rise of private penance made it easier to link the two, especially in the practice of the Celtic Church, where penance was initially related to the work of the "soul friend."[15] With the spread of private penance, it became more common for direction to occur in the confessional. Today, among Roman Catholics and Anglicans alike, there is concern that spiritual direction be distinguished from sacramental reconciliation, but not necessarily separated from it. That is, spiritual direction deals with more than just repentance and absolution, but cannot exclude them.

The confessor—who may or may not be one's spiritual guide—is in an excellent position to help discern blocks and obstacles in a Christian's spiritual journey; some of these may well be removed by absolution. Confession further involves a disciplined reflection on one's own concrete behavior, matching it against the standard of Christ's call. Tilden Edwards, in his use of the image of the spiritual director as physician, locates the use of sacramental reconciliation as part of cleansing the wound, because it links moral and spiritual accountability for and awareness of personal actions and their consequence, purge guilt, and empower a sense of reconciliation and caring with self, God and neighbor."[16]

In Kenneth Leech's definitive work on spiritual direction, *Soul Friend*, a lengthy appendix is devoted to the relationship between spiritual direction and the sacrament of Reconciliation. The latter finds its place in the former because, "the life of the Spirit is both initiated by, and characterized by, *metanoia*, repentance, transformation, and an integral element in spiritual direction is the maintaining of a continuous repentance nd sorrow for sin."[17] Leech deplores the frequent Anglican isolation of Reconciliation, calling for its restoration to the mainstream of pastoral care, the variety of activities through which the Church pursues its ministry of reconciliation. These include preaching and liturgy, Baptism, Eucharist, ministry to the sick, and other ways the Church reaches out to individuals in their concrete situations. He concludes,

> The hearing of confessions then cannot be isolated from the total reconciling work of the church, and it only makes sense in that context. The confessional stands at the critical point between liturgy and life, the positions adapted in worship and those which prevail in social life.[18]

Martin Thornton likewise argues that, kept in proper perspective, sacramental confession is an important part, but only a part, of a relationship of spiritual guidance:

> Practice and experience ... suggest that, for those truly intent on spiritual growth, the old adage "none must, all may, some should" virtually translates itself into "none must, all should."[19]

As a means of enabling continuous repentance and conversion, measuring our behavior against our convictions, worshipping and opening ourselves to God, removing blocks and obstacles in our paths, and facing our own dishonesty and self-delusion, Reconciliation is a significant aid to spiritual growth. Ascetical theology and spiritual direction provide a context for the sacrament and are enriched by it. The grace of Reconciliation may help us undertake the spiritual journey and give us the strength we need to persevere. For, let us make no mistake about it, the journey is an arduous one, and we will need all the help God's grace can supply in order to undertake it. As Urban T. Holmes wrote,

> There seems to be a reluctance on the part of many of us to get on with the journey. We read the masters with hesitance and are often surprised to find them fascinating. Why the reluctance or hesitance? Is it possible that we fear we might indeed hear a call from God that summons us from our comfortable place, for our Ur of the Chaldees, to go serve him? It has been said that we need to be careful about what we pray for: we might get it. It should be added that we need to beware, for if we listen to God we might hear him, and what he says may well make us uncomfortable. But it can also make us whole.[20]

Psychological Theories of Human Development

As we noted above, Karl Rahner has suggested that it may be helpful, in spiritual direction, to have some schema to help us know more fully the "vital situation" of individuals as they seek to grow in the Christian life. This entails a "psychology of age groups and life experience" which, at one level, illuminates our understanding of the human subject. Certainly, it is part of the pastoral task to be familiar with concepts, theories, and data from the human sciences that seek to do just that. Our basic conviction is: if we would explore the divine-human encounter inherent in Christian life, and in the sacraments in particular, we would do well to know as much as we can about the human side of the encounter. We will want to know more about how people develop their natural capacities for understanding, judgment, and action, all of them part of the sacrament of Reconciliation. There is a huge body of literature devoted to this concern, and we will attempt a very selective overview of material from the social sciences, and especially various branches of psychology.

There is a helpful means of organizing the material from the social sciences in a little book which deserves to be better known in religious circles than it is, *Roots of Caring, Sharing and Helping*, by Paul Mussen and Nancy Eisenberg-Berg.[21] Their concern is with "pro-social behavior," which they define as follows:

> Pro-social behavior refers to actions that are intended to aid or benefit another person or group of people without the actor's anticipation of external rewards. Such actions often entail some cost, self-sacrifice, or risk on the part of the actor. A wide variety of behavior is encompassed by this rubric, including generosity, altruism, sympathy, helping people in distress by giving material or psychological assistance, sharing possessions, donating to charity, and participating in actions designed to improve the general welfare by reducing social injustices, inequalities or brutality.[22]

This, in secular language, would seem to be the heart of what Christians understand as appropriate action in the world and highly relevant to our discussion of the sacrament of Reconciliation.

Mussen and Eisenberg-Berg identify three main families of research and theory that bear on the matter of pro-social behavior: psychoanalytic theory, cognitive-developmental theory, and social learning theory. The first two are widely known in the religious community; the third is less familiar. All are rich in pastoral resources. We will see more explicit appropriations and elaborations of this literature by theologians and ethicists, especially in the increasingly prominent field of "faith development."

Psychoanalytic Theories

The rich and varied stream of psychoanalytic theory begins with the work of Sigmund Freud. All modern theories of personality development must begin with his work, even though there are few orthodox Freudians today. In this approach, the personality is constructed of id, ego, and superego. These components of personality develop primarily in early childhood through a series of psychosexual stages—the oral, anal, phallic, latency, and genital—that have their characteristic conflicts. Most significantly for our interest is the development of the superego, which is the internalization of moral standards and the force behind moral conduct. The superego develops out of the ego at about age three to five, from the introjection of parental standards and the resolution of the Oedipus conflict in identification with the same-sex parent. It enforces its standards by stimulating the ego's feelings of guilt or pride. The subsystems of the superego include the ego ideal, which sets positive standards, and the conscience, which judges and regulates behavior through negative sanctions. This teory of personality is most illuminating when it deals with the development of guilt and shame and the internalization of prohibitions; it is less adequate in explaining altruistic or pro-social behavior.[23]

Freud's first major critic and reviser was Carl Gustav Jung, whose influence in religious circles has increased in recent years. Jung's theory of personality structure and development is too complex for extensive treatment here, but certain themes are worth highlighting. First, Jung suggests a much longer time of development than does Freud, and he leads us to a life-span view of personal growth. Throughout that span, the key concept is that of individuation through growth of a fully differentiated, balanced, and unified personality. The systems of the personality become more complex, enabling a much richer response to the environment. This occurs when the individual becomes more and more conscious of the various subsystems that underlie his or her personality and are often in conflict. Through integration and transcendence the opposites are unified and the self is discovered as a new center of personality. Individuation, according to Jung, occurs through four periods—childhood, youth and young adulthood, middle age, and old age—and in the later stages becomes more and more a spiritual process. For our purposes, Jung is helpful in directing attention to the whole of life as the arena for individuation and the development of greater consciousness.[24]

Although there have been many other theorists in the Freudian succession, the most important for the present task is Erik Erikson, whose work has had considerable impact on the religious community. Denoting his approach as "ego psychology," Erikson's concern has been the life-long development of the person through eight "epigenetic" stages. In each of these stages, the interaction of physiological and social demands precipitates a "crisis" requiring resolution for continued healthy development of the personality. Each crisis contains, as it were, polar tendencies, and its successful resolution gives rise to an ego quality that enhances the personality. Appendix C summarizes Erikson's developmental theory. Both in its life-span approach and its clear conceptual descriptions of the epigenetic stages, Erikson's work illuminates human development and has given rise to some interesting further research and theory.[25]

Having stated an appreciation for Erikson's work and that of others in the psychoanalytic tradition, I must, however, add a note of caution. These theories are just that—theories—and they are long on concepts and short on data. They are based on conclusions reached by their formulators out of their own introspection, observations of life at large, and the experience of a relatively small number of people, usually patients in psychotherapy. There has been very little empirical research done on these theories, and it is highly ambiguous. Further, with the exception of Jung, they all tend to commit the male-as-normative fallacy—they define human personality in the terms of men's experience while regarding women as aberrant.

We may not, then, conclude that such theories are factual, empirically verifiable by the usual scientific methods. Whether or not they may be true, that is, representing some ultimate reality beyond the evidence of the senses, is essentially a matter of faith. These theories, and especially that of Erikson, are useful primarily as heuristic devices, stimuli for asking the right questions. In pastoral practice, for example, Erikson's epigenetic stages may assist exploration of the significant issues an individual may face at his or her particular place in life. They may provide a map useful in helping to trace a person's life journey, but we must always acknowledge that they may may be inaccurate and that each indi-

vidual's journey is unique. In pastoral ministry, to be an Eriksonian (or Freudian or Jungian) fundamentalist is likely to be a
considerable liability.

Cognitive-Developmental Theory

In the cognitive-developmental school, we encounter a field
of psychology where data are plentiful indeed. Many of its phenomena and theoretical constructs have been subjected to
empirical verification. There is a trade-off, however, in that this
research concentrates on a much narrower "slice of life" than does
psychoanalytic theory, as it focuses on the act or process of knowing. Admittedly, this is no small thing, but neither is it the whole of
what it means to be human. The "grand old man" of this field is
the Swiss psychologist Jean Piaget, whose talent for collecting data
"in the wild" and synthesizing useful concepts made him one of
psychology's authentic geniuses. The basic contributions of
Piaget, Piagetians, and neo-Piagetians will, in all probability, stand
for some time to come, despite their limitations. Robert Kegan has
stated the limitations rather elegantly.

> With very few exceptions, the work of the Piagetians ("neo" or
> otherwise) must still be charcterized as about *cognition*, to the
> neglect of *emotion*; the *individual*, to the neglect of the *social*; the
> *epistemological*, to the neglect of the *ontological* (or concept to the
> neglect of being); *stages* of meaning-construction, to the neglect of
> meaning-constitutive *process*; and (forgive the awkward expression
> of this last) what is *new and changed* about a person, to the neglect of
> *the person who persists through time.*[26]

Most of Piaget's foundational work was done by giving various
kinds of tasks to children and watching their performance, or by
asking them questions and analyzing their responses. In the area
of general cognition these observations led Piaget to posit four
basic stages of development: sensorimotor, preoperational, concrete operational, and formal operational. Sensorimotor charac-
terizes infancy (birth through two years of age), when the child
"knows" only through his or her senses and movements. In the
preoperational period of early childhood (roughly ages two
through seven), language is acquired and joined to thought, which
is a kind of manipulation of mental pictures in a rather limited

way. In the preoperational phase children are egocentric in their thinking and limited by their perception. At about seven, they begin to acquire the ability to manipulate symbols and engage in logic. These manipulations, called by Piaget "operations," enable the child to make generalizations and take the perspectives of others. This stage is called "concrete operational" because the child has not yet achieved the ability to manipulate more abstract concepts. Abstract reasoning comes in the early teens, as the stage of "formal operations" is reached and the individual's cognitive abilities are by and large complete, although some adults never reach formal operations.[27]

In the 1960s, Australian Christian educator Ronald Goldman attempted to apply Piaget's general cognitive theory to the "religious thinking" of children and adolescents. His research indicated children's difficulties in properly understanding the Bible stories and religious concepts before they were cognitively "ready" to do so. Goldman recommended sweeping changes in Christian education curricula, including a more naturalistic and experiential approach for younger children, avoidance of much Biblical material until children were older, and, in general, what he called a "child-centered" approach to religious instruction.[28] Goldman's work received some attention by American Christian educators, and some materials, such as the Morehouse-Barlow "Readiness for Religion" series, were developed to incorporate his ideas. Goldman's theories illustrate the limits of the Piagetian approach, however—it helps us take seriously the cognitive structures involved in religious knowing, but only that. As John Westerhoff said to me when I asked him about Goldman, "That's fine, if you believe that religion is primarily a cognitive phenomenon; I don't."

Early in Piaget's career, he wrote a work specifically relevant to our study, *The Moral Judgment of the Child*. Not only did he begin investigations of moral development, but he developed some of the methodology still being used. He interviewed children of different ages, told them stories, and asked them questions about rules, authority, right and wrong, punishments and rewards, cooperation and competition among people. His analysis of the responses led him to develop a three-stage model of the understanding of rules, moral judgment, and the sense of justice. The stages are heteronomous morality (the morality of constraint or moral realism), intermediate morality, and autonomous morality (the morality of cooperation or moral relativism). This developmental sequence is hierarchical and holds for all normal children, according to Piaget. Cross-cultural empirical research has demonstrated that the stages hold in most cultures.

The first stage is found in children in the preoperational stage of cognitive development. These children regard rules, obligations, and commands as "givens"; they are external and unchangeable. Justice is whatever authority figures or the rules command, and wrongdoing is judged according to the letter, not the spirit, of the law. Children at this stage believe in "immanent justice" (for example, God will make something happen to you if you hit your sister) and that values are absolute, either right or wrong without ambiguity. Acts are evaluated on the basis of their consequences, with little or no consideration given to the actor's motivations or intentions. These phenomena are rooted in the child's egocentrism and realism of thought and are fostered by adult authority.

The second stage is transitional and results from a greater interaction with peers and the discovery of a more egalitarian way of relating to others. A sense of fairness and equity reduces the appeal to authority and is seen, for example, in the notion of "reciprocal punishment" (the punishment should fit the crime). This stage in moral development parallels the development of concrete operations in general cognition.

The most mature stage, autonomous morality, comes with adolescence. Equity dominates the understanding of justice, and a wrongdoer's motivation and intentions, as well as extenuating circumstances, are considered in making judgments. Rules are seen as a kind of social contract that can be modified or abolished by mutual consent. This stage comes about, Piaget believes, primarily because of peer interactions in which there is no *a priori* authority like that of the parent. Children become able to cooperate, act reciprocally, and take the perspectives of others about whom they are much more concerned.[29]

Piaget's theory of moral development has been extensively

elaborated, developed, and tested over twenty years by Lawrence Kohlberg of the Harvard School of Education and his associates. This body of research, and a variety of critiques of it, form the foundation of any investigation of moral development. Kohlberg began by posing a series of "dilemmas" to boys aged ten through sixteen and, with probing questions, analyzed the kinds of reasoning they used to solve them. The reasoning was more important to the final theory than the actual solutions. The most famous Kohlberg dilemma is that of Heinz:

> In Europe, there was a woman near death from a special kind of cancer. There was one drug that the doctors thought might save her. It was a form of radium that a druggist in the same town had recently discovered. The drug was expensive to make, but the druggist was charging ten times what the drug cost him to make. He paid $200 for the radium and charged $2000 for a small dose of the drug. The sick woman's husband, Heinz, went to everyone he knew to borrow the money, but he could get together only about $1000, which is half of what it cost. He told the druggist his wife was dying, and asked him to sell it cheaper or let him pay later. But the druggist said, "No, I discovered the drug and I'm going to make money from it." So Heinz got desperate and broke into the man's store to steal the drug for his wife. Should Heinz have done that? Was it actually wrong or right? Why? Is it a husband's duty to steal the drug for his wife if he could get it no other way? Would a good husband do that? Did the druggist have the right to charge that much where there was no law actually setting a limit to the price? Why?[30]

In analyzing the data, Kohlberg developed a six-stage model for moral reasoning, summarized in Appendix D. These stages are defined, following Piaget, according to the following criteria:

1. Stages imply distinct or qualitative differences in children's mode of thinking or of solving the same problem at different ages.
2. These different modes of thought form an invariant sequence, order, or succession in individual development.
3. Each of these different and sequential modes of thought forms a "structured whole." A given stage response ... represents an underlying thought organization which determines responses to tasks which are not manifestly similar.
4. Cognitive stages are hierarchical integrations. Stages form an

> order of increasingly differentiated and integrated structures to
> fulfill a common function.[31]

Research tends to confirm that the attainment of a particular stage
of reasoning and thinking is a necessary, though not sufficient,
precondition for the parallel stage of moral development.[32]

Virtually all researchers and theorists who have commented
on Kohlberg's work admit its profound significance in providing a
conceptual framework to shape our understanding of how people
make certain kinds of moral judgments. Nonetheless, Kohlberg
has his critics, and we will attempt to survey some common themes
in their criticism, both from the point of view of academic psycho-
logists, and from those within the religious community, Finally, we
will examine in depth an astute feminist critique and revision of
Kohlberg's theory of moral development.

A central criticism of Kohlberg, endemic to any cognitive
approach to human thought and action, is simply that Kohlberg's
work is on moral judgment, which may not show any very clear
linkage to moral action. We may know how the subjects *reason*
about hypothetical moral dilemmas, but we do not know how they
act when faced with a concrete situation. Further, the dilemmas
tap only reasoning about competing claims and the application of
rules; they do not show any development of "pro-social" reasoning, that is, how to judge a situation involving a conflict between
one's own needs and those of others. For example, Nancy Eisenberg-Berg used a methodology similar to Kohlberg's to develop a
sequence of pro-social moral reasoning reported in Appendix E.

Criticisms of Kohlberg's work have also been made from a
theological point of view. Many of these center on his reduction of
moral development to problems of justice only. As William
Rogers, of the Harvard Divintiy School, puts it:

> From a religious point of view this becomes especially important if
> we are interested in the moral importance not only of how we think,
> but of how life and behavior are transformed by the power of a
> centering *relationship* of faith, fidelity or religious transformation.[33]

Further, Kohlberg's irreversible stages do not seem in accord with
our actual experience of moral regression and do not take into
account sin and the presence of intractable evil in the world.

Finally, as is true of most of the cognitive-developmental literature, Kohlberg's theory is highly individualistic and pays little attention to the social or religious context of oral judgment and action.[34]

One of the most interesting offshoots of Kohlberg's work is a thorough critique and revision of it by Carol Gilligan, one of his research associates and a fellow Harvard faculty member. Although devoid of any specifically religious references, her *In a Different Voice* makes fascinating reading for Christian reflection.[35] Gilligan surveys the literature of personality theory and development and finds that male development is consistently taken as normative. According to these theories, growth is achieved as people become more separate and autonomous yet women are raised to be empathic and to place primary concern for relationships. Thus,

> when the focus on individuation and individual achievement extends into adulthood and maturity is equated with personal autonomy, concern with relationships appears as a weakness of women rather than as human strength.[36]

The male-as-normative fallacy marks the work of Kohlberg, who, it may be recalled, developed the stage theory out of his interviews with *boys*. Gilligan finds that women are consistently scored as being at lower stages of moral development on his dilemmas. Yet, on re-analysis and in further research, she finds their moral reasoning to be not so much inferior as different.

This research has led Gilligan to contrast two styles of moral reasoning. Kohlberg's stages, based on justice as the central principle, form a style characteristic of males. Females, on the other hand, tend to reason according to the principle of caring relationships, yielding a different focus.

> This conception of morality as concerned with the activity of care centers moral development around the understanding of responsibilities and relationships, just as the morality of fairness ties moral development to the understanding of rights and rules.[37]

The content of responses discloses the use of different images by males and females: hierarchy versus network, reasoning by categories versus reasoning by context, individuation by separation versus individuation by connection. Thus,

the moral judgments of women differ from those of men in the
greater extent to which women's judgments are tied to feelings of
empathy and compassion and are concerned with the resolution of
real as opposed to hypothetical dilemmas.[38]

Gilligan is led by her analysis to postulate three stages of
moral development for women, roughly parallel to Kohlberg's
overall progression from preconventional through conventional
to postconventional moral judgment. Put simply, it is a progression from selfishness to responsibility or goodness to a fully
developed ethic of care.

The sequence of women's moral judgment proceeds from an initial
concern with survival to a focus on goodness and finally to a
reflective understanding of care as the most adequate guide to the
resolution of conflicts in human relationships.[39]

I am struck by how this line of reasoning parallels contemporary
Christian moral and pastoral theology, with its concern not just
for law but for people. The correlations with our previous discussion of the theology of Reconciliation should be obvious.

Much of Gilligan's original research was done on women's
decisions about abortion. This may, indeed, be the feminine moral
dilemma *par excellence*. It illustrates both women's concern with
real problems and their efforts to balance the need of mature
adults to accept and take responsibility for their actions against
that concern for relationship and care.

When a woman considers whether to continue or abort a preg-
nancy, she contemplates a decision that affects both self and others
and engages directly the critical moral issue of hurting. Since the
choice is ultimately hers and therefore one for which she is responsible, it raises precisely those qualities of judgment that have been
most problematic for women.[40]

One might say that men debate and agonize over whether abortions should be permitted, and women debate and agonize over
whether or not to have one. As Gilligan shows, this is an issue on
the cutting edge of any contemporary consideration of how people think and act morally.

Although Gilligan's methodology is not without flaw and her
conclusions may make too much of gender differences, her work

adds a great deal to Kohlberg's. Future work on moral development, and any appropriation of that work by theologians, must
take into account both approaches to moral judgment. Certainly,
any Christian moral theology will need to address itself to both
justice and care (or love), and the working out in the socio-political
arena of both rights and responsibilities. The experience of both
men and women is needed as the raw material for any adequate
moral theology and ethics, and we have much to learn from each
other. Surely, Gilligan is right in her hopes for a future integration.

> To understand how the tension between responsibilities and rights
> sustains the dialectic of human development is to see the integrity of
> two disparate modes of experience that are in the end connected.
> While an ethic of justice proceeds from the premise of equality—
> that everyone should be treated the same—an ethic of care rests on
> the premise of nonviolence—that no one should be hurt. In the
> representation of maturity, both perspectives converge in the real-
> ization that just as inequality adversely affects both parties in an
> unequal relationship, so too violence is destructive for everyone
> involved. The dialogue between fairness and care not only provides
> a better understanding of relations between the sexes but also gives
> rise to a more comprehensive portrayal of adult work and family
> relationships [and, we might add, the whole social order].[41]

The most helpful contribution of cognitive-developmental
theory, especially in its concern with morality, may well be the
convincing demonstration that moral judgment does, in fact,
develop. As people grow, they see greater complexities to moral
issues, are more able to take the perspectives of others, and find
that their resources for decision making are more interior than
imposed from without. The work of Kohlberg and others is useful
as a map, or sketch, of a likely direction for human moral cognition and reasoning to take; however, Christians will want to take
the *content* of one's moral convictons rather more seriously and to
test the way these convictions are expressed in action. Possibly,
Kohlberg's *summum bonum*, Stage 6, with its emphasis on equality
and human rights, while commendable is rather less than the
sacrificial love to which we are called by the example, death, and
resurrection of Jesus.

Social Learning Theory

Our final field in psychology presents us with both abundant data and a concern for what people actually do. Indeed, social learning theorists are largely uninterested in motivation, conscious or unconscious, or even in cognition and reasoning. They are concerned with observable moral action, or what is called "prosocial *behavior*." Such behavior is, to oversimplify, the consequence of direct reinforcements (rewards), originally from parents, teachers, or other authority figures, that become learned and internalized. Pro-social behavior seems to be shaped by learning and conditioning, observation and modeling, or imitation, all described by the term "socialization." Such behavior derives from a number of antecedents, among them biological factors, group membership and culture, socialization experience, cognitive functions, and situational determinants. Of these, socialization experiences are probably the most important factors.[42]

How do these other factors assist in the movement from moral judgment to moral actions? Mussen and Eisenberg-Berg find that "stage or level of moral judgment is a significant, although not very powerful, regulator of the individual's propensity to behave pro-socially."[43] According to many social learning theorists, the primary mediating factor is empathy. Empathy has three components, two cognitive and one affective: the ability to discriminate and label the affective states of others, the ability to assume the perspective or role of another, and emotional responsiveness to another. The role of empathy in mediating pro-social behavior has been subjected to considerable research, the results of which tend to confirm the hypothesis.[44] The cognitive aspects of empathy can it seems, be trained like any other cognitive skill; this has significant implications for Christian nurture and formation.

The social learning approach does not tend to generate "grand theories," and much work is yet to be done on prosocial behavior. Nonethelesss, some tentative conclusions useful to pastoral ministry may be offered. After a survey of hundreds of studies, Mussen and Eisenberg-Berg conclude that:

The children who will spontaneously donate some of their own

possessions to poor orphans or volunteer to assist classmates who
are injured or upset . . . are likely to be relatively self-confident and
active children, advanced in moral reasoning as well as in role-
taking skills and empathy. Altruists are likely to be the children of
nurturant parents who are good models of pro-social behavior, use
reasoning in discipline, maintain high standards, and encourage
their children to accept responsibilities for others early.[45]

While this statement may be lacking in theological depth, it
does indicate that behavior consistent with Christian norms may
be shaped by the family or the community. Couched in traditional
language, it points to things which Christians have known for
centuries: the imitation of Christ and the saints (models), ascetical
and moral theology (reasoned discipline), the demands of membership in the Body of Christ (high standards), and the mission
and ministry of each Christian (accepting responsibility for others). Social learning theory, in its emphasis on observable acts,
neglects the whole interiority of the human creature, but Christian doctrine asserts that acts matter. Although social learning
theory lacks an understanding of sin, it points to some factors
which, in an individual case, may contribute to moral failure.
Finally, it suggests that the relationship between cognition and
action is not one-way only. As a friend of mine once put it, we don't
just think our way to new actions; we can also act our way to new
understandings. In our response to the call of Christ, both thinking and acting are very important.

The Growth and Development of Faith

The social sciences, and especially psychology, may provide
us with methodology and conceptual frameworks for examining
human experience but, of themselves, they cannot point to the
dimension of depth that is the realm of religious understanding.
This latter is the task of theology in its various forms. I want to
proceed now to some consideration of the interrelationship of
psychology and theology, with special attention to the notable
"grand theory" in this area, the faith developmental approach of
James Fowler. We can illustrate this relationship by a brief consid-

eration of morality and religion. This focus is fruitful because morality has been considered at great length both by social scientists and by moral theologians and ethicists.

From the psychological perspective, an article written for the First International Conference on Moral and Religious Development by F. Clark Power and Lawrence Kohlberg provides insights. Power and Kohlberg suggest we look at the psychological unity of religion and morality provided by the ego.

> Insofar as religion serves to strengthen the self which makes moral decisions, it has an effect, not on the particular moral judgment, but on whether any judgment is to be made and whether or how, if it is made, that judgment will be carried into action.[46]

This can be done in three ways:

> 1) A religious interpretation of one's life as a vocation can renew one's sense of moral purpose and commitment, 2) religion can serve to encourage the self confronted by the abyss between the moral ideals of the self and the injustice of the world, and 3) a religious perspective can heighten one's moral sensitivity by offering a vision of the self as intrinsically related in a familial bond with other selves.[47]

To test their hypotheses, Power and Kohlberg took some of Fowler's data (see below), and analyzed it with their methods. They concluded that:

> Moral judgment is a necessary but not sufficient condition for religious reasoning, at least in the higher stages. Moral reasoning appears to provide the basic concepts of justice and care, out of which a theistic notion of God can be fashioned. God is never known directly but always mediated indirectly through human experience. It is only by being able to form concepts of ordinary socio-moral [experience] that we can qualify them in a way to point beyond to the extraordinary—to God.[48]

This research also led them to a concern for the development of "just communities" where the values of morality and religion can be nurtured and supported. Further research should, in their opinon, consider the relationship between the individual and the shared belief of the community. They conclude that "the ontological function of religion is to provide a courage of par-

ticipation which sustains community in confrontation with pri-
vatism and totalitarianism."[49]

While Power and Kohlberg take what might be called the
inductive approach, reasoning from human experience to the
transcendent, a movement in the other direction is also possible.
Enda McDonagh, writing on "Moral Theology and Moral
Development," sees the relationship of religion and morality as
"creative interaction."

> Distinct but inseparable for Christians, they provide mutual chal-
> lenge and correction as well as illumination and confirmation. The
> conversion to the human other (person and community) which
> characterizes moral activity encounters also the mystery of the
> Ultimate Other as mediated by the human. The further reach of
> moral activity is prayer. The turning to the Ultimate One demands
> and empowers the recognition of and response to its incarnate
> presence in the neighbor(hood).[50]

One might well ask at this point if it is possible to take all these
approaches, theories, and concerns and develop one coherent
account of how one other meets the Ultimate Other in that most
human activity we call faith. It would seem a daring adventure,
requiring remarkable gifts of creativity and synthesis. We find this
in the work of James W. Fowler.

Fowler's Stages of Faith

In the period from 1972 to 1981, James Fowler and his associates conducted lengthy interviews with 359 people. In the course
of two to two-and-a-half hours, they were asked questions about
the course of their lives, life-shaping experiences and relationships, present values and commitments, and religious beliefs
and experiences. From these interviews, Fowler was able to
develop a model of "stages of faith." The model represents not
only an analysis of the data, but also an attempt to synthesize the
work of Erikson, Piaget, and Kohlberg, among others.[51] Fowler
defines faith as:

> The process of constitutive-knowing
> Underlying a person's composition and maintenance of a com-
> prehensive frame (or frames) of meaning
> Generated from the person's attachments or commitments to cen-

ter of supraordinate value which have power to unify his or her experiences of the world
Thereby endowing the relationships, contexts, and patterns of everyday life, past and future, with significance.[52]

According to Fowler, there are six stages of integrated patterns, which build on each other and incorporate into more elaborate structures the patterns of the previous stages. The stages are thus both structural-hierarchical (as in Piaget) and functional-sequential (as in Erikson).[53]

The infant begins life in a pre-stage of *undifferentiated faith*. The seeds of trust, courage, hope, and love are fused in an undifferentiated way and are founded on the basic trust and relationship with the one(s) providing primary love and care. This time of life is largely inaccessible to empirical research. Undifferentiated faith can be endangered either by a childish fixation on narcissism or on the failure of caregiver(s), leading to isolation and failed mutuality. The transition to Stage 1 begins with the development of thought and language opened by the use of symbols in speech and ritual play.

Stage 1, Intuitive-Projective Faith (ages three to seven). This is a time of fantasy and imitation. The child is influenced by example, moods, actions, and stories of the visible faith of primary adults. Thought-patterns are fluid and imaginative, unrestrained and uninhibited by logical thought. The imagination produces powerful and long-lasting images and feelings, both positive and negative, to be sorted out and reflected on later. The stage of first self-awareness, it is ego-centric in its perceptions of others. At this time comes the first awareness of death and sex and the strong taboos with which family and culture surround them. The emergence of concrete operational thinking mediates the transition to Stage 2.

Stage 2, Mythic-Literal Faith (school age). At this stage, a person begins to appropriate the stories, beliefs, and observances that symbolize membership in his or her community. These beliefs are interpreted literally, as are moral rules. Symbols are taken as one-dimensional and literal in meaning. Story, drama, narrative, and myth give coherence to experience. Figures in narrative are anthropomorphic, and the person can be affected powerfully by symbolic and dramatic materials. There is no ability, however, to step back from the narrative and formulate reflective, conceptual meanings. Children at this age can more accurately assume the perspective of others, and they construct a world of reciprocal fairness. This stage is typical of the school-age child, but can continue on into adolescence and even adulthood. The transition to formal operational thought breaks down literalism and allows reflection on meanings, leading to Stage 3.

Stage 3, Synthetic-Conventional Faith (adolescence). The adolescent's world opens up and faith must find a coherent orientation in the midst of a much more complex life experience that includes family, school or work, peers, media, and perhaps religion. The ultimate environment is structured in interpersonal terms deriving from the experience of personal relationships. It is a "conformist" stage, tuned to the expectations and judgments of significant others, without a sufficient sense of autonomous identity necessary to construct an independent perspective. Beliefs and values are deeply but unreflectively held and rarely examined. The person in Stage 3 has an "ideology," a relatively consistent cluster of values and beliefs, but he or she has not examined nor become fully aware of it. Those holding different values or beliefs are perceived as being different "kinds" of people. Authority is located in those holding traditional authority roles, if they are felt to be worthy, or in the consensus of a valued, face-to-face group. The adolescent or adult can become fixed at Stage 3. If so, he or she is in danger either of so internalizing the values and expectations of others as to have no basis for autonomous judgment and action, or of being driven to despair or a sense of meaninglessness by a perceived betrayal by significant others.

The transition from Stage 3 to Stage 4 is a particularly critical one. It may be mediated by clashes with authority figures, marked changes in what had been seen as immutable standards, experiences requiring critical reflection on the changes in one's own beliefs or values, or the discovery of the relativity of such beliefs or values. For many, this comes about in the experience of leaving home, emotionally or physically. As the individual moves toward

Stage 4, he or she must face the significant and unavoidable tensions of forming an autonomous identity, appropriating values, beliefs, and actions as one's own, and wrestling with the deep questions posed by life. In short, one must assume responsibility for who one is and who one is becoming.

Stage 4, Individuative-Reflective Faith (young adulthood). The self, which has been sustained by others, now claims its own identity as a distinct and unique person. To sustain that new identity it adopts a frame of meaning which is consciously differentiated and aware of its own boundaries and inner connections. Self (identity) and outlook (world view) become acknowledged factors in responses to one's own actions and those of others. This is a "demythologizing stage" in which the person has a definite set of meanings, often symbols translated into concepts, that makes conscious and explicit the person's intuitions about the ultimate environment. The person at Stage 4 is capable of critical reflection on his or her identity and outlook, but risks a stultifying rationalism or a "second narcissism" as everything is assimilated into his or her world view. The rationalism of Stage 4 tends to inhibit awareness of or reflection on unconscious factors influencing judgment or behavior. Although this stage is most appropriately found in young adulthood, many adults never reach it, or do so only in their thirties or forties. Disillusionment with one's own compromises, the discovery of unassimilated material from the unconscious, or the realization that life is more complex than previously understood may mediate a transition to Stage 5.

Stage 5, Paradoxical-Consolidative Faith (mid-life). The person in Stage 5 has come to terms with defeat and his or her own past, and is ready to integrate much that was previously suppressed or unrecognized. What Ricoeur calls "second naïveté" is developed, and symbolic power is reunited with conceptual meanings in an opening to one's "deeper self." One is alive to paradox and the truth in apparent contradictions and seeks to unify opposites in mind and experience. At this stage, the person is ready for closeness to anything different and threatening, and there is a universalized commitment to justice. The seriousness of mid-life allows

energy to be spent in helping others generate meaning and identity. Ironic imagination develops as the capacity to see and be in the
most powerful meanings of one's own life or group, while realizing
that they are relative, partial, and possibly distorted. The person in
Stage 5 can appreciate symbols, myths, and rituals (one's own and
others'), having been grasped by the reality they represent. He or
she has a vision of an inclusive community of being and thus
keenly sees the divisions in the human family. Stage 5 is rarely
found before mid-life, and is divided in loyalty between an
untransformed world and a transforming vision. In a few souls,
this division yields to the call of radical actualization in Stage 6.

Stage 6, Universalizing Faith. In such people, their felt sense of
ultimate environment is inclusive of all being. With a "contagious
faith," they create zones of liberation from the social, political,
economic, and ideological shackles placed on the future. They live
in felt participation in a power that unifies and transforms the
world, and are experienced as subversive to the ordinary structures of life. Such persons often die at the hands of those they hope
to change and may be more honored and revered after their death
than during their lives. They have a special grace that makes them
seem more lucid, more simple, more fully human than the rest of
us. Although their community is universal, particularities are
cherished because they are vessels of the universal. Life is both to
be loved and held loosely. Such persons are ready for fellowhship
with persons at any of the other stages and from any other faith
tradition. Persons do not achieve Stage 6; it a grace and a gift.

In each of these stages, Fowler sees an integration of these
operational aspects: form of logic, role-taking, form of moral
judgment, bounds of social awareness, locus of authority, form of
world coherence, and symbolic functioning.[54] Parallels with other
theorists are drawn, as illustrated in Appendix F. Even in this brief
summary, Fowler's faith development theory is exceedingly complex and erudite. Given how much it seeks to integrate, this is not
surprising. As Fowler says, however, beyond all the abstractions
and technical language, the theory is an expression of the human

search for the One who is the end of all our yearning. The role of the faith community in this quest is crucial.

> Faith communities must discover how to meet people as *whole* beings, embracing their hearts as well as their minds, their bodies as well as their souls. We must enable people to name and recognize their hungers and their real depth. Forms of spirituality, community celebration, testimony, and shared action in faith can then emerge which will sustain a humanizing common life. Such faith communities are indispensable for the human family's well-being.[55]

Understandably, Fowler has his critics, although they recognize the significant integration and creativity of his theory. William Rogers, who is typical of Fowler's critics, makes the following observations. There is no essential criterion for establishing the normative object of faith (God). The methodology, a mix of inductive and deductive, risks artificially imposing categories on open-ended data. There are inadequate links to perceptual and symbolic theory, so that we are not sure how perceptual processes give form and meaning to experience. The insights of depth psychology are not adequately included.[56] From a Roman Catholic point of view, James O'Donohoe faults Fowler for not taking seriously the meaning of revelation in faith and for tending to imply that growth in faith is something one does, rather than being a matter of grace. O'Donohoe sees Kohlberg and Fowler as more concerned with the process of moral judgment and faith development than their goals, and wonders how human development of faith leads to conversion.[57] Fritz Oser distinguishes Fowler's concern for "faith" from "religious judgment," which is more specific in its content and orientation, and elaborates a stage theory of the latter as a matter of the relationship of God and man.[58]

Other Approaches to Faith Development

Two Anglican theologians, John Westerhoff and Urban T. Holmes, have developed schemas for Christian growth that help put Fowler's work in perspective by showing slightly different ways of conceptualizing the same process. They do not have the database of Fowler's work and are, therefore, more speculative. They use somewhat different theological starting points, are explicit in their Christian content, and define faith in different ways. Both assume what Holmes calls "sublation," that is, that we carry the characteristics of each stage or style of faith into the next. Westerhoff uses the growth rings on a tree as a metaphor for this process.

In *Will our Children Have Faith?*, John Westerhoff writes out of a concern for the education of Christians through an interaction of the faith community with the individual. He calls this "faith enculturation." For him,

> Faith . . . is a verb. Faith is a way of behaving which involves knowing, being and willing. The content of faith is best described in terms of our world view and value system, but faith itself is something we do. Faith is an action. It results from the actions of others, it changes and expands through our actions with others, and it expresses itself in our actions with others.[59]

Westerhoff discerns four sequential "styles" of faith: experienced faith, affiliative faith, searching faith, and owned faith.[60]

Experienced faith is the faith of childhood. We learn, in childhood, about faith from the actions of others, especially as they relate to us. It is not so much a matter of words spoken, but the experiences we have connected with those words. It results from our interaction with other faithing selves, and especially parents. Affiliative faith normatively develops in early adolescence and is the faith derived from a conscious belonging to a faithing community. It is nurtured by participation in that community's activities and is characterized by the dominance of the religious affections, which are nurtured especially by the arts and are usually more important than the intellect. At this stage, one learns by intuition. Affiliative faith also has a strong sense of the authority of a community and its story.

Under optimal conditions, late adolescence becomes a time of searching faith, when one must test the faith received by experience and affiliation. Searching faith is characterized by doubt and/or critical judgment, experimentation, and a need for commitment to persons and causes. It is more rational and seeks a reason for values and beliefs. If the needs of searching faith are met, in early adulthood one may move to owned faith, usually through what has been historically called conversion. One's faith commitments become a part of one's identity, and one seeks to witness to them in word and deed. Owned faith is a radical and personal response to the demands of the Gospel, lived out in community.

As in other developmental models, Westerhoff allows for the possiblity of becoming fixated, of ceasing to grow, at any of the stages/styles. He notes that most adults have their faith arrested at the affiliative style. Westerhoff argues that every church needs a variety of approaches to education at all age levels and that it is necessary to provide experiences to help people move on to the next stage. This can be particularly aided or retarded by the church's rites of transition. A ritual for "blessing" the transition to searching faith would be especially valuable and is usually absent. Westerhoff's model shows its origins in a concern for education, which make it highly suggestive for any approach to Christian formation, nurture, and spiritual growth.

In *Turning to Christ*, Urban T. Holmes draws on Fowler, Westerhoff, Richard of St. Victor, and John Wesley for his theory of Christian growth. He calls for a renewed concern for sanctification in Christian theology and practice, as it was so vividly expounded by Wesley.[61] Our understanding of the process of sanctification can, in his opinion, be enriched by a theory of Christian growth, as long as we do not become rigid about it and allow our concepts to limit the activity of the Holy Spirit. Holmes thus writes of three "ages" of spiritual growth: the ages of imagination, reason, and understanding.[62]

The age of imagination is infancy and childhood, Fowler's Stages 1 and 2 and their parallels in Erikson and Piaget. It is a time when the "I" emerges as one differentiated from the world, becoming aware of subjects and objects. Imagination is the primary cognitive style for relating to the world and is defined by Richard of St. Victor as "the contemplation of God in the world of the senses." Imagination becomes the root means of religious knowing, but in time it must be subjected to the scrutiny of reason. The age of reason is adolescence and early adulthood, and its principal task is adaptation to external reality. At this time people make distinctions and comparisons and are not particularly self-conscious. Holmes finds that this age encompasses Fowler's

Stage 3 (which is parallel to Westerhoff's affiliative faith) and
Stage 4. According to Holmes, the danger of Stage 3 is "fideism,"
the confusion of subjective feelings with objective truth. Stage 4 is
the threshold of Christian maturity: here one develops a certain
autonomy that, for example, makes spiritual direction a possibility.

Finally, by grace, one reaches the age of understanding, the
time of mid-life characterized by Fowler as Stages 5 and 6. At this
time, one must give up one's illusions, make and test new choices
in life, and confront and integrate certain profound polarities
within oneself. Understanding is, according to Richard of St. Victor, God's self-disclosure to the person who is open to Him, not a
knowledge we achieve but one given to us. Holmes observes that
not too many attain this kind of understanding, but he dares to
hope that if sufficient attention is paid by the Christian community to issues of spiritual direction, evangelization, and renewal,
this vision of spiritual maturity may become more and more
normative.

A Model of Christian Growth For Pastoral Practice

The search for useful material from related disciplines has led
through a survey of the literature of spiritual direction and
ascetical theology, psychology (especially psychoanalytic, cognitive-developmental, and social learning theories), and the growing field of faith development. At this point, it may be useful to
step back and ask what we have found in each that might be most
useful in informing the pastoral task, especially with respect to the
sacrament of Reconciliation. The working pastor need not necessarily master all the intricacies of each body of literature, but he or
she may extract certain useful themes and know where to go for
further resources. The art of being a pastor (and it is an art) can
nonetheless benefit from an acquaintance with a wide variety of
theoretical and scientific disciplines that serve to guide and shape
its practice.

From the literature of spiritual direction and ascetical theology, comes an appreciation of the Christian life as a call to

perfection and a growth in holiness. This takes place especially through prayer (a progressive opening to the presence of God) for which the Threefold Way of purgation, illumination, and union is a helpful map. Growth in prayer is enabled by discernment and the spiritual disciplines, of which the sacrament of Reconciliation is an important aspect.

The psychoanalytic tradition, and especially the work of Erik Erikson, can alert us to ways the person grows and develops in the natural capacity for psychic integration and relationship. Erikson's epigenetic approach gives a helpful description of this growth process. He calls upon us to look across the life-span for growth, directing our attention to the role of "crises." These crises are described as a working through of opposite tendencies which, if managed in a healthy manner, produce certain ego strengths, almost virtues.

From the cognitive-developmental literature, especially that of Piaget and Kohlberg, we gain an appreciation of the epistemological processes at work in the growth of persons. Faith is, among other things, a way of knowing, and it is useful to have theoretical models of how we know, reason, and judge. We might note, in passing, that the biblical word for judgment, *diakresis*, also gives us the notion of discernment, a very important activity in spiritual direction. Cognitive-developmental theorists make clear that certain capacities must be present before certain activities can be undertaken. The work of Kohlberg and Gilligan provides us with two complementary foci of moral reasoning—concerns for justice and care—that, taken together, give a vision of moral maturity and have clear implications for Christian ethical judgment and action.

Social learning theorists help us to ask questions, not just about judgment and reasoning, but about action and behavior. Their strategies for the shaping of behavior have implications for Christian nurture. This body of research is particularly useful, for it raises the issues of role-taking, empathy, modeling, and socialization. The latter category has parallels to John Westerhoff's faith enculturation paradigm for Christian nurture.

The standard in the area of faith development is the massive integrative work of James Fowler, with his emphasis on stages of faith as a search for and structuring of meaning to give coherence and purpose to human experience. John Westerhoff's model of styles of faith directs our attention to the interaction of the individual with the faith community. Finally, from the work of Urban T. Holmes, we can see how synthesis can be constructed that relates much of the above to classical concerns of theology, notably the Holy Spirit's work of sanctification and the tradition of ascetical theology as seen in the work of Richard of St. Victor.

In seeking to synthesize all this material, I find myself drawn almost inexorably toward yet another stage model of Christian growth. Perhaps the evolutionary paradigm is endemic to human understanding, or maybe it's just that such conceptual frameworks are easier to manage. However, some preliminary comments and cautions may help avoid overstating the case or making too much of the framework. Such a framework is only a map, a sketch, a heuristic device. The tests of any model are (1) how usefully it describes our experience and (2) how fruitful are the questions and insights it evokes.

Two critics of Kohlberg and Fowler, Robert Kegan and Stanley Hauerwas, demand that we attend to the processes and realities underlying any developmental model. Kegan notes that any developmental model works at the level of subject-object, or self-other differentiations. He argues, however, that "below" these differentiations there is a persisting phenomenon we might call the "deep structure," a context that gives rise to self-other differentiations and which he calls "meaning-constitutive evolutionary activity." As Kegan puts it simply, "persons are not their stages of development; persons are a motion, a creative motion, the motion of life itself."[63] Kegan would have us attend to this creative motion; he finds it manifested particularly in three phenomena: the tension between our drives for attachment and separation, the recurring experience of losing and recovering meaning, and the universal need to be recognized. Tillich calls this creative motion the "ground of being," and Fowler labels it "the ultimate environment." Against this ground the figurative play of stages is to be seen.

> When the constructive-developmental paradigm makes not the
> stages the focus but their relation to the process which subtends and
> creates them, then the paradigm directs us anew to those rhythms

of death and rebirth," fall from grace, loss of innocence, eviction from paradise, return and repentance, the leap of faith, saving grace, redemption—those rhythms we find in the hot centers of human history, where men and women have found ways to see beneath the dust of daily life.[64]

Stanley Hauerwas also argues for a view of Christian life that transcends a series of developmental stages. He evokes the language of spiritual growth, holiness, and perfection we have encountered before. Moral action in the world is, for Hauerwas, a matter of "character" and the acquisition and practice of the "virtues." The underlying theme giving coherence to life is described as "narrative." For the Christian, character is made up of all our stories and achieves fulfillment insofar as it is joined to the great narrative, the Christian story of the life, death, and resurrection of Jesus.[65] As we work through a model of growth, we will do well to keep our eyes fixed on that underlying motion, the narrative to which we are joined by Baptism, and the basic Christian insight that growth and identity are not achievement but gift.

> Finally, to be holy or perfect suggests more radical transformation and continued growth in the Christian life than can be captured by the idea of development. For the convictions that form the background for Christian growth take the form of a narrative that requires conversion, since the self is never fully formed appropriate to that narrative. Thus the story that forms Christian identity trains the self to regard itself under the category of sin, which means we must do more than just develop. Rather Christians are called to a new way of life that requires nothing less than a transvaluation of their past to reality.[66]

Hauerwas's concern with conversion raises it as a second preliminary issue to our developmental synthesis. Does the extensive body of literature we have surveyed have anyting to say about this most important aspect of the Christian life? It may, especially when we look at the process in any developmental model by which persons move from one stage to another. John Westerhoff is quite explicit about it, stating that the "movement from affiliative faith through searching faith to owned faith is what historically has been called *converson*."[67] This process of conversion is, it would seem, motivated by a sense of radical discontinuity and challenge to one's prior beliefs, values, and actions. The developmental literature repeatedly uses this language in describing the process of moving from one stage to another.

An illustration can be found in the work of Carol Gilligan. In the follow-up portion of her study of women's decisions about abortions, she consistently found that the experience had a profound effect on the woman's subsequent moral development. Such a crisis, she concluded, both revealed and created character, and provided the occasion to face the truth about oneself and one's relationships.[68] She describes her findings:

> In my research on people's judgment and resolutions of actual experiences of moral conflict and choice, these experiences were often described as precipitating a crisis in moral understanding. The awareness of contradictions between judgment and action or of a disparity between intention and consequence led to a period of questioning and doubt which had the hallmarks of a stage transition. My interest in the role that life experiences played in late adolescent and adult moral development was initially spurred by retrospective reports of students in the college sample who identified their confrontation with real moral dilemmas as turning points in their conceptions of self and morality.[69]

Enda McDonagh, surveying the same phenomenon from a Christian perspective, concludes that:

> In the contexts of both community and evil, or moral action as interaction and good action as also overcoming some evil, the development takes the form of conversion. It is in the traditional senses a conversion *from* (evil and self-centeredness) and a conversion *to* (good and the other). It should be the conversion of person and community.[70]

This logic suggests an interaction between transition (from one stage or style) and conversion. I suspect that the process can go in either direction. Further, we might conceive of sacramental reconciliation as a kind of ritualized crisis, a confrontation with both the truth of oneself and the proclamation of divine love, which, by its nature, is capable of mediating personal, moral, or spiritual growth.

This theme is also elaborated by Robert Kegan. In the flow of what he calls the meaning-constructive evolutionary activity, we need ways of "remembering" the "deep structure" underlying our growth, or, in Hauerwas's terms, of remembering the narrative that is the source of our character. It does not seem too farfetched to describe this as an *anamnesis* of, in Westerhoff's marvelous phrase, "who we are and whose we are." In a faith community, this often occurs through the sacraments, or as Kegan trenchantly states it:

> In a community worthy of the name there are symbols and celebrations, ritual, even gesture, by which I am known *in the process of my development*, by which I am helped to recognize myself. Intact, sustaining communities have always found ways to recognize that persons change and grow, that this fate can be costly, and that if it is not to cost the community the very loss of its members, then the community itself must be capable of "recognition."[71]

In the Christian community, this "recognition" and the grace to bear it can be found in Reconciliation.

Our final preliminary concern is stated in Urban T. Holmes's concluding observations on Christian growth. He notes that there is no particular value to the various stages: a person at Stage 5 is not "better" than one at Stage 3. Any growth in our capacity for relationship with God is tempered by our willingness to make use of the capacity. Second, justifying grace is present in all stages, and faith enables the relationship with God wherever we may be in our pilgrimage. Holmes calls for "space for grace" that allows us to respond to whatever God has to offer to the extent of our capacities. He believes that if there is such space where we can respond to and cooperate with God, we will naturally grow in grace. Such growth is not a self-improvement plan, but a response to the love of God that always nurtures and seeks us.

> The intrinsic-imaginal space is, therefore, the place of grace. Grace is nothing less than the presence of God himself. God's presence to us is not that of a despot, but of a love. Love must have space in which to move and invite the beloved.[72]

What follows is an attempt at synthesis. It is not based on any primary data, but rather seeks to put together a number of theories, many of them with extensive bases in empirical research. This is a speculative effort and will only be valuable as a guide or map to the unfolding of an explicitly Christian life and identity.

Rather than dignify the constituent parts with the name "stages," let us rather refer to "patterns." We assume that these patterns sublate, that we carry characteristic modes of thinking, reasoning, being, and acting from one pattern into the other, with frequent "regressions" to the modes of a previous pattern. We move from pattern to pattern by natural growth, evolution, crisis, and conversion. How we live in each pattern is governed and modified by a number of individual variables, such as personality type (used in a Jungian sense), gender, socialization experiences, affectivity, and intellect.

In formulting each pattern, we ask certain distinct, yet overlapping, questions and borrow terms from a wide range of sources. What is the locus of control from which we derive our faith, moral judgment, and so on? Is it relatively exterior or interior? What is the form of our relatedness? How do we regard and interact with others? What kind of intimacy do we establish? What is our relationship to community, especially the community of faith? What is our cognitive style? What psychological issues are most salient to us in a given pattern? What form does our spirituality take? Allied to this are our understanding of sin and images of God. At what stage of faith, in Fowler's terms, do we find ourselves in each pattern? Put together, I find four patterns emerging for our religious identity: heteronomous, conventional, autonomous, and theonomous.

In a *heteronomous* pattern of religious identity, the locus of control is to be found in what Fowler calls our "primal others." It is "they" oriented, and "they" are usually parents, immediate family, or a few significant others with whom we have intense relationships. The others in our lives are, more or less, "givens," objects for our gratification; intimacy is limited and primarily familial. Our relationship to community is characterized by what Westerhoff calls "experienced faith" which is consistent with pre-operational cognitive functioning. We face the psychological issues of the first four stages of Erikson's theory, which we can collectively call individuation. Our primary task is to become a self-consciously distinct person, capable of hope, will, purpose and competence.

In the heteronomous pattern, our spiritual style is relatively undifferentiated. We are not yet enough of a self to begin a spiritual pilgrimage in any real sense. God is one of the "givens," and prayer is a kind of intuitive being with what is. Sin is considered a kind of disobedience to authority, and our understanding of sin is largely undeveloped. Our images of God are mythic, polytheistic, or animistic. This is the faith of early childhoood, which moves from being undifferentiated, through Fowler's Stages 1 and 2. It is possible for this pattern of religious identity to persist into adulthood, but if it does, the person will remain a spiritual child and not, I think, in the positive sense commended by Jesus.

The *conventional* pattern of religious identity is characterized by a limited expansion of our horizons. The locus of control is still exterior, still a matter of "they," but the significant others are now one's group, society, or nation. We continue to relate to most others as objects, now somewhat conceptualized through categorization or stereotyping; it is a matter of "us versus them," with some limited capacity for intimacy. Our relationship with a community is one of conscious belonging; the affiliative style predominates. Cognitively, this pattern is based on concrete operations with the beginnings of formal operations. The central psychological issue is that of identity formation issuing in fidelity.

In the traditional Threefold Way, persons in the conventional pattern begin purgation. Indeed, this pattern is likely to be characterized by a strong sense of sin as breaking the rules or violating the norms. One's image of God is likely to be "henotheistic"—there is one God, but he is the God of one's particular group. We belive in the God of the Americans, or of the Episcopalians, or of the bourgeoisie. Fowler's Stage 3, "synthetic-conventional faith," dominates this pattern, as it gives it its name. I agree with Holmes that this is the standard pattern of religious identity among American church-people, and it is quite possible for it to last a lifetime.

As Fowler notes, the transition to an *autonomous* pattern is a critical one—it represents a kind of threshold of religious maturity. The locus of control is interiorized and faith, moral judgment, and the rest now become matters of "I." We relate to others in mutual respect; we recognize that they have rights and are persons in themselves, not just objects for our gratification. On this basis, real intimacy becomes possible. In the forging of this identity, we may need to take leave of our community, or at least subject its norms to scrutiny and analysis. This is Westerhoff's searching faith, moving to some degree of owned faith. It is in this pattern that the issue of intimacy or isolation becomes crucial and we begin to be able to love. Later, we may also be involved in the tension between generativity and stagnation that can lead us to care.

Spiritually, this pattern represents a growth from purgation to illumination. We move from being beginners to proficients, in prayer from novices to journeymen. Our understanding of sin becomes more personal; we see it as the violation of relationships, the betrayal of mutuality, with self, neighbor, and God. Images of God may be difficult to grasp; we confront the divine hiddenness that can lead us to mature monotheism. If I am who I am, then God is who God is, too. Though not full maturity, this "individuative-reflective faith" is a foretaste of mature Christian identity, and a reasonable goal for many people.

I have taken from Tillich the term *theonomous* for the fourth and final pattern because it seems to represent the full maturity of biblical religion. The locus of control is interior, but arises from a deepened interiority that is profoundly in touch with the Ultimate; it is "I, yet not I, but Christ in me." Its form of relatedness is solidarity, a universal intimacy based on one's recognition of all others as fellow beings-in-God. In relationship to community, this is the essence of owned faith that chooses to abide in the Body, with all its imperfections, because one meets the Spriit there. Cognitively, theonomous faith is paradoxical: the fruition of formal operational thought is the ability to hold and affirm the seemingly contradictory. Psychologically, there is an expansion of care and, with age, the triumph of integrity over despair, leading to wisdom.

In this pattern, one's spiritual piilgrimage leads through further illumination and, by grace, may attain to some measure of union. This is contemplative lifestyle; a Benedictine abbot I know has called it "two beings being together." The sense of sin is transmuted and much less anxious; and sin is understood as a refusal to become. Life is seen as gift, and sin as unwillingness to accept all that is offered. In this pattern, Fowler's Stage 5 is reached, and perhaps those especially called to it may even attain Stage 6. In a theonomous pattern of Christian identity we arrive, and yet do not arrive, at what the author of Ephesians calls mature [person]hood in Christ. The journey is not finished, it always continues, but deeper and deeper, higher and higher, until the consummation in glory.

The passage form autonomy to theonomy is largely the work of the second half of life, of a time when the individual faces the waning of energy and the nearer approach of death. Among psychological theorists, Jung gave special attention to this part of life and to the importance of individuation in it. This is a process in which the ego, one's relatively superficial identity, can be transmuted into the much richer self by integrating into consciousness much of what has been hidden within one's psyche. Later-life individuation involves the reconciliation of opposties, an appropriation of subconscious archetypes and the development or deepening of religious consciousness. Individuation, in Jungian terms, partakes of the paradoxical quality of Christian understanding: the self is at once achieved and yet is discovered, or received, as a gift.[73]

We may see in this evolution an almost cyclical pattern beginning in undifferentiated unity with the All, proceeding through individuation to autonomy, and then returning to a new unity, but a unity that encompasses the polarities of life in God's cosmos. At each stage, in each pattern, there is, if we allow it, room for growth and relationship with the One who is the Alpha and the Omega, our Creator, Redeemer, and Sanctifier. To use Augustine's marvelous term, it is a process of becoming truly what we are.

> With the drawing of this Love and voice of this Calling
> We shall not cease from exploration
> And the end of all our exploring
> Will be to arrive where we started
> And know the place for the first time....
> —T. S. Eliot, *Little Gidding*

V

Reconciliation in Pastoral Practice

HAVING surveyed the historical development of the sacrament of Reconciliation, explicated its contemporary liturgical treatment, and developed a synthesis of various pastoral resources, we are now ready to turn to its actual use in pastoral ministry. In this chapter, then, I want to discuss the pastoral context of Reconciliation, especially in Anglicanism, suggest ways a developmental approach might illuminate pastoral practice, and conclude with a discussion of how people can be prepared for Reconciliation and how it is appropriately celebrated and administered. I do so in the firm conviction that we can only approach *any* aspect of pastoral ministry with an appropriate grounding in theory and theology. The Church does not need a handy "how to do it" manual for confessors, any more than it needs an extensive guide to the arrangement of the furniture for the sacrament. What is needed is a good pastoral practice informed by theory, and theory derived from theological reflection on practice. This is, I believe, what pastoral theology is all about.

The Pastoral Context of Reconciliation

For Anglicans, a principal element in the pastoral context of Reconciliation is its voluntary nature. Time and time again, we are reminded by all commentators in this tradition that the maxim is, "all may, some should, none must." Thus, persons will come for the sacrament, not out of any sense of being compelled to by canon law or even normative piety, but out of some felt personal need. They may have some sense of compulsion if, for example, they have been schooled in the Anglo-Catholic view of "The Christian's Obligations," but, even here, such an ascetic is really essentially *chosen*.[1] It may be appropriate, therefore, to consider what sort of people are most likely to seek sacramental reconciliation. At the risk of stereotyping, let me suggest three probable cases: the Prodigal, the Perplexed, and the Pilgrim.

The Prodigal is one who has, for some length of time, truly left the Church. Urban T. Holmes tells the story of a man, raised in the Church, who left it in the course of pursuing medical and psychiatric studies. Years later, as he was walking down a city street, he saw a sign outside an Episcopal Church announcing that confessions were being heard. Drawn by some incomprehensible power, he found his way into the confessional, knelt down and sobbed, "I want to come home."[2] For such a person, the Sacrament of Reconciliation will be a powerful symbol and means of a return home, a reconciliation with God and the Christian community. Such a turning-repentance-conversion is a reclaiming of one's Baptism, of which Reconciliation is a powerful *anamnesis*. As such, it may be sufficient in itself, or it may prove a helpful preparation for the "Reaffirmation of Baptismal Vows" with the laying-on of the Bishop's hands (*BCP*, p. 419). Sacramental Reconciliation has always been the Church's way of saying, "welcome home" to one who has "wandered far in a land that is waste" (*BCP*, p. 450).

The second type, the Perplexed, represents, in a way, the classical Anglican case for Reconciliation. This is the one of whom the 1548 Prayer Book spoke:

> And if there be any of you whose conscience is troubled and grieved in anything, lacking comfort or counsel, let him come to me, or to some other discreet and learned priest taught in the law of God, and confess and open his sin and grief secretly. . . .[3]

Throughout the Anglican tradition it is clear that, whatever other use the rite may be put to, this one is unquestioned. It is not uncommon for a pastor to find someone deeply troubled by a particular act or issue, needing assurance and healing. That person may be healed and strengthened by Reconciliation. Such a "one-issue" confession would certainly have the weight of Anglican tradition behind it. An example might be the case of abortion. Reading the accounts Carol Gilligan gives of the agony of decision suffered by women, weighing the conflicts with self and others, balancing rights and responsibilities, I found myself asking where the word of grace might be found. It is no accident, I think, that the General Convention statement on abortion refers quite specifically to sacramental Reconciliation as appropriate in this case.

> That in those cases where it is firmly and deeply believed by the person or persons concerned that pregnancy should be terminated for causes other than the above [a threat to health; probability that the child will be deformed; rape or incest], members of this Church are urged to seek the advice and counsel of a Priest of this Church, and, where appropriate, Penance.[4]

Finally, and I suspect this will be most common in pastoral practice, there is the Pilgrim. This is the person who is consciously and conscientiously seeking a deeper knowledge of God and a more faithful Christian life through spiritual discipline and direction. We have already discussed the relationship between Reconciliation and spiritual direction and need only mention it here. Virtually all writers on spiritual guidance and ascetical theology agree that this sacrament has an important place in the intentional Christian pilgrimage, for sin is the primary obstacle on our path to perfection.

Each of these cases requires different pastoral tactics, but I believe these can be comprehended in an overall pastoral strategy. Such a strategy includes at least three elements: an understanding of the nature of the pastoral task, the community as a whole, and the minister of Reconciliation (in Anglicanism, the priest).

The Nature of the Pastoral Task

In the usual fashion of the *via media*, pastoral ministry in Anglicanism has usually included elements from both the Catholic and Protestant approaches. At the risk of oversimplifying, the Catholic approach emphasizes the pastor as minister of the sacraments, and the Protestant approach emphasizes, at least in our day, the minister as professional. Each approach has its strengths and deficiencies. The sacramental approach grounds pastoral work in an incarnational understanding of the Church and links it to the Church's life as a worshipping community. Pushed too far, however, the sacramental approach extracts Christian life from the real world and turns the Church into what one of my friends calls "a sacrament mill." The professional model of ministry, on the other hand, emphasizes meeting people where they are and developing skills to be of real help, particularly counselling skills. The professional model tends to be untheological and rather reductionist, grounded almost exclusively in a psychological understanding of pastoral care. That most Protestant seminaries have one position in "pastoral care" devoted almost exclusively to counselling suggests an excessive emphasis in this direction. We need an understanding of the pastoral enterprise that comprehends both the sacramental and the professional emphases, and more.

A very important book in this regard is Don Browning's *The Moral Context of Pastoral Care*. Arguing from a Protestant point of view, Browning criticizes the tendency to focus on counselling at the expense of moral guidance, on adjustment to the culture at the expense of a prophetic critique of the culture.

> Pastoral care deals with what ministers have done to promote two principal functions: 1) the incorporation of new members and their discipline in the goals and practices of the Church, and 2) the assistance of persons in handling certain crises and conflicts having to do with existential, developmental, interpersonal and social strains.[5]

Browning finds that pastoral ministry has tended to concentrate on the second function, ignoring the first—the *cura animarum*, the cure of souls.

Surverying the Hebrew Scriptures and the New Testament, Browning discerns a tradition of spiritual guidance with prominent ethical dimensions. Jesus stands in this tradition as a moral teacher, a *supralegalist* who takes the law as given but seeks to plumb its depths to find its inner meaning. Jesus spoke extensively on the disciplines of the life of the Kingdom of God, and pastoral care in his name will need to nurture Christians in those disciplines. Browning argues for pastoral care committed to practical moral guidance, with the recognition that the norms of the Christian Church are often at significant variance with those of the culture.[6]

I affirm Browning's analysis and suggest that Reconciliation stands exactly at the intersection of the various approaches to pastoral ministry. It enables the minister to deal with the issues of Christian discipline and the handling of personal crises, to provide practical moral guidance without imposing unbearable burdens, and to administer sacramental grace so as to inform and transform a Christian's life in the world.

Clebsch and Jaekle found four functions of pastoral care to be present, in different concentrations, throughout Christian history: healing, guiding, sustaining, and reconciling. Although Reconciliation has been variously identified with one of these functions, usually healing or reconciling, ideally it draws together all four.[7]

The Reconciling Community

An adequate contemporary sacramental and pastoral theology must involve a recovery of a sense of the Body of Christ in all aspects of ministry and Christian life, and this is especially true with respect to Reconciliation. Concern with the ecclesial aspect of the sacrament is one of the notable features of much recent theology on the subject. The Christian community is, thus, an integral part of the pastoral context of this sacrament, as well as of pastoral care in general. Pastoral care is not just something pastor and "client" do in the privacy of the study, nor is sacramental reconciliation only a matter for the "little box." The Church is the community to which pastor and penitent alike belong, and from which they both derive their identity. Further, pastoral care is not only for individuals, but can be directed at groups, congregations, and institutions. Indeed, all of these can be not only the objects of pastoral care, but its instruments as well. With respect to Reconciliation, the Church is called to be at least three things: the community of moral discourse and formation, the community in which reconciliation is experienced, and the community that cele-brates and proclaims reconciliation in the world.

Browning describes the Church as a center for moral dis-course and decision-making, the historical bearer of the "ethical sensibility" permeating the larger society, and a place where the ethical capacities of the rest of society can be stimulated and shaped.

> The task of the church is to construct an *ethical* world, a world in which forgiveness and renewal simultaneously are pos-sibilities.... [This] means that the church, in an effort to perform both its general religious task and the task special to its own histor-ical tradition, must create, maintain, modify and re-create the value symbols of its ethical visions.[8]

In this effort, the "community of moral discourse" seeks to embody the tradition and apply it in the context of rapid change. Central to that task is a dialogical preaching, a "method of sum-marizing, enriching and further stimulating the ongoing moral inquiry of the worshipping community."[9]

In order to do this, the community must develop a "sense of style," that is, a sense of "the way we people are" so that the community of discourse can become a community of action.[10] This is, I believe, what John Westerhoff means when he delineates the "faith enculturation community" paradigm of Christian edu-cation and nurture. The paradigm requires

> examining and judging our total life as a community of faith to see how well we live and transmit our Christian story or tradition, how well we minister to the total needs of whole persons in community, and how well we prepare and motivate individuals and communities to act on behalf of God's coming community in the world.[11]

Roman Catholic moral theologians have also moved in this direc-tion since Vatican II. The Church's role is seen not in "laying down the law" but in "forming a responsible people." Recognizing that persons live socially and communally, there has been a renewed concern for the moral formation not just of the individual but of the community itself.[12]

Needless to say, if the community does not act out this con-cern for moral formation and forgiveness within its own life, it is not likely to persuade either its members or the world of the validity of its moral vision. Thus, it is an important aspect of the pastoral enterprise to lead the community to own and act on the norms it professes. Christians need to be especially sensitive to one another, recognizing in each sister or brother a fellow redeemed sinner struggling to be faithful to the call of Christ. Mutual exhortation, support, concern, and forgiveness have been signs of the Church's vitality since the earliest days. Tad Guzie and John McIlhon have commented on the sacramental functions of communal penance services, but their comments have implications for the wider life of the Church as well. These functions are to make explicit what is implicit in any Eucahrist, "that the Church exists for no other purpose than to be a community of reconciliation, a body of reconcilers"; to work against our tendency to repress guilt by awakening a communal sense of sin; and to "provide a context in which personal guilt is joined with reflection on communal responsibility and thus kept from turning in on itself."[13]

Preeminently, the Church does this through ritual and sacrament. These seek to embody the values the community deems important and to present them vividly to its members for their appropriation. In this way also, those values are celebrated, proclaimed, and represented to the world. Forgiveness is central to moral inquiry, for without it we can easily fall into despair at our puny efforts to live up to our convictions. As Browning puts it:

> If the relationship between forgiveness and moral inquiry is properly understood, it means that Christians should have the courage to pursue the goals of moral life with assurance. If they miss the mark, or if they falter, forgiveness is a possibility and through this they can be renewed again to pursue the moral course. Forgiveness makes the moral life possible. It frees us to pursue the moral life with a minimum of stultifying guilt and sense of defeat. But without assuming the seriousness of the demand of Christianity for ethical inquiry and conduct, forgiveness loses its meaning and its renewing power. [Thus], central to ritual in the Christian community should be the dimension of forgiveness.[14]

The demand for moral effort, and the grace of forgiveness, are both manifested in powerful ways in the sacrament of Reconciliation. As Leonce Hamelin observes, this rite serves two functions at the same time:

In one, the *entire community* is invited to celebrate the gift of reconciliation; in the other, certain Christians ask the Church to celebrate
with them the gift of *their* reconciliation.[15]

The Priest as Confessor

It is appropriate to remember that the sacrament of Reconciliation is essentially a corporate act, but, at the same time, it is
ministered on behalf of the Body by one person. Hamelin states
that relationship very well:

> It is the prayer of the community—but, clearly, an assembly that has
> a priest as president and leader—that causes the voice of Christ to
> ring in the Father's ears. At times, the priest may be alone when he
> fulfills the role of bearing witness to the conversion of sinners and
> giving them the sign of forgiveness; nonetheless, by reason of the
> fact that he is a minister, he has the ecclesial community with him.[16]

We, therefore, need to ask what sort of a person the minister of
confession needs to be, how he or she understands and goes about
this ministry, and what factors the confessor must attend to.

The ministry of Reconciliation is both part of the general
work of the priest and a specialized ministry. All priests are, by
virtue of ordination, authorized to administer the sacrament;
some have conspicuous gifts for it and are more likely to make it a
significant part of their ministry. Kenneth Leech puts it very well:

> It is impossible to teach men to become "good confessors," for the
> qualities which go to make for effectiveness in the ministry of
> absolution are simply those which go to make for holy and compe-
> tent priests and pastors. The "good confessor" is a priest who is
> steeped in prayer, disciplined in his life, acquainted with human
> frailty and endowed with the gifts of wisdom, and the knowledge of
> the ways of the Spirit.[17]

Monika Hellwig states cogently the particular tasks of this general
ministry: to pray with and for the penitent; to listen with deep
compassion on behalf of God and the community; to discern the
spiritual state of the penitent; to convey the forgiveness of God;
and to help express the exigence of God's call to conversion.[18]

In order to provide some focus to our consideration of how
one most fruitfully exercises this ministry, let us look at the priest
first as the celebrant or president of Reconciliation, then under

the complementary images of parent and friend, judge and physician, guide and fellow-pilgrim. Finally, we need to consider the meaning of the Seal of Confession.

Although it is perhaps less obvious and public than in the celebration of the Eucharist or the administration of Baptism, the priest in Reconciliation acts as celebrant or president. In this, he or she acts as one who presides on behalf of the assembly, proclaims the Word of God, and leads the prayers of the people of God. In this way, the priest and the community make *anamnesis* of the mighty work of Christ in reconciling individuals and the world to God. The ministry of the whole Body is thus focused by the priest, acting as what Holmes calls "a sacramental person," or as Crichton puts it, "a sign in himself, a sign of the Father's love shown forth in the Son."[19]

The ministry of presiding is that of calling the assembly together, enabling each member to perform his or her particular liturgy, and seeing that all is done "decently and in order."

> The president of any liturgical act, especially the sacrament of penance, sets a tone and creates an atmosphere which is both settling and calming. If the sacrament of penance is par excellence a sacrament of peace, the president of that action must be above all a man of peace. The peaceful, calming, and settling manner of the confessor will be remembered far longer than any other aspect of the pentitent's confession.... Good presidential action is essential to good liturgy. At the very least it is good manners; and at the very most it is wholeness, and that's the doorway to holiness.[20]

Liturgical presidency is incarnational; that is, the personal qualities of the individual minister also manifest the presence of Christ.

> The authority of the confessor and spiritual director resides in the fact that they represent the community of the Church. They represent it in virtue of their ordination; they are the present and concrete expression of the authority of Jesus Christ who alone possesses the power to forgive.... Sacramental confession and absolution derive their efficacy only from Christ, who confers ecclesiastic authority upon his minister.[21]

This authority is evoked by the proclamation of the Word of God in power. The ministry of proclamation is essential to ordination and establishes a link between the present moment and the whole history of God's saving work. The forgiveness of sins is a central aspect of the Good News, the Gospel, which is at the heart of the Church's proclamation. Above all, we proclaim the redemptive presence of the Word made flesh.

> By proclaiming the life-giving word of God and celebrating the signs of salvation that restore or intensify this life, the pastor makes present the Christ who is God's concrete presence within the human race.[22]

It is, finally, always true that the president of the Christian assembly is one who leads it in prayer. The ministry of Reconciliation is a powerful act of intercession and mediation. The sacrament must, therefore, always be administered in a profound spirit of prayer. The confession is a prayer to God for forgiveness and restoration, and it is the confessor's task to lead the penitent in this prayer. At the same time, the confessor joins his or her prayer to the penitent's, and their mutual prayer is joined sacramentally to the prayer of the whole Body of Christ. Sacramental Reconciliation is a specific case of the general Christian imperative to pray unceasingly to God for the world and for one another. This is also symbolized by the traditional request of the confessor to the penitent, "and of your charity, pray for me, a sinner."

Any act of Christian intercession effectively places the intercessor "in the middle," and this is particularly true of the ministry of Reconciliation. The confessor stands with the penitent as she or he approaches God, but also stands with God and his Church in speaking the truth in love to the penitent. Thus, the priest must identify profoundly with the weakness and sin of the penitent, which the confessor shares, while, at the same time, standing in and for the tradition that bears the Good News. In this, our model is the ministry of our Great High Priest, who is not "unable to sympathize with our weakness, but one who in every respect has been tempted as we are, yet without sin" (Hebrews 4:15). This ministry has been expressed in the tradition by many complementary images that manifest the paradoxical nature of the divine-human ecounter.

A central image of the confessor as spiritual father appears repeatedly in the tradition. In the late twentieth century, we might wish to avoid this image on the grounds of authoritarianism and sexism. As Kenneth Ross observes, it has been regrettably common to associate spiritual paternity with a kind of Victorian fatherhood—distant, stern and unsympathetic. I join with Ross in rejecting this view, and emphasize instead the gentleness and sacrificial love inherent in a genuine paternity after the image of God.[23] The relationship of confessor to penitent must avoid all efforts at domination and control, without losing any of its strength. As Thurian puts it:

> The spiritual fatherhood of the confessor...consists not in an authority which might be in danger of becoming possessive...but rather in his duty to exhort with gravity, to console with gentleness, and seriously to adjure believers, in order to bring them to God's Kingdom and glory.[24]

The rather more serious problem with the image of spiritual father is its exclusion of women. I once heard it said that an Anglo-Catholic bishop argued against the ordination of women by saying, "But how ridiculous! Can you imagine entering the confessional and saying, 'Forgive me, mother, for I have sinned?'" Well, in our human history, I suspect most of us have said something like that any number of times! As Carol Gilligan has forcefully argued for the inclusion of women's experience in any theory of moral development, so I believe that the experience of women as confessors will greatly enrich our experience of this sacrament. Maternal authority and love are no less powerful than fatherly care in evoking the best that is in us. Thus, we may do better to think of the ministry of the confessor as a parental one, expressed in various ways by particular confessors—male and female.

As a parent, I recognize my ministry as calling forth the best that is in my children, enabling them to become more fully the persons God has made them to be, not objects for my gratification, but wonderful bearers of the *imago dei*. My love for my children, when freed from possessiveness and a need to control, is a disinterested love that delights in their uniqueness; it is a love that, by grace, serves them in their growth. Raymond Studzinski, O.S.B., has found just this sort of care in the relationships of the Desert Fathers to their disciples. These wise counsellors were known, not for their judgmental rectitude, but for their humility and compassion, their twin commitment to patience and truth.

> The concerns of the Desert Fathers throughout their confessional method was that their disciples might patiently come to discover the truth of themselves. . . . Above all, the spiritual father was one who had learned to love. He possessed a love which, because it regarded the other as another self, had enough humility and reverence to approach the inner life of another without violating it or treating the other as an object.[25]

This same parental care can be found, Studzinski suggests, in the *Rule* of St. Benedict, by which generations of abbots and abbesses nurtured the men and women in their communities in their growth in holiness.[26]

An integral part of the parental ministry of Reconciliation is acceptance. As a parent tells a child, "I may not always like what you do, but nothing can ever make me stop loving you," so the confessor assures the penitent that no sin can ever ultimately separate us from God, if we will turn again and receive the divine mercy always awaiting us. I remember my own father sending me off to college and urging me to talk to him and my mother about anything that happened there. "Son," he said, "your mother and I have seen a lot of life, and while some things might surprise us, I don't think anything could shock us." The confessor needs to be able to hear whatever the penitent has to say without shock or embarrassment, so that the accepting love of God may be made known. Kenneth Leech observes that, in this context, the laying-on of hands in absolution makes perfect sense as the appropriate gesture of the affection of a parent for a beloved child.[27]

Even this revisionist view of spiritual parenthood is subject to abuse, and needs to be balanced. Some commentators suggest that the ministry of the confessor is also the ministry of a friend. Studzinski has found this theme in the warm and gentle "affective educational" direction of St. Francis de Sales, for example. This approach includes an interpersonal warmth and responsiveness, respect for the freedom of the individual, and a self-effacing willingness to let the penitent play the major role in discerning

God's call. It is expressive of the rubric in the new *Rite of Penance*, "The priest should welcome the penitent with fraternal charity and . . . address him with friendly words."[28] The confessor as friend sits loosely on sacramental authority, preferring to be present with the penitent.

> To relate in a brotherly or sisterly way is also, of course, to make oneself more vulnerable, more accessible, more subject to comparison and challenge, more easily put on the spot, less easily able to hide one's person behind the role and function. . . . In the sisterly or brotherly role one must stand before others in the simplicity or poverty of one's own being, and therefore one must minister out of one's own poverty and weakness and not out of the strength of an institutional status.[29]

This is consistent with the ministry of Jesus, who said to his disciples,

> No longer do I call you servants, for the servant does not know what his master is doing; but I have called you friends, for all that I have heard from my father I have made known to you. (John 15:15)

Just as Jesus has been seen as the judge of all persons, so, too the image of confessor as judge has been very much part of the tradition. With the movement away from the juridical emphasis in Reconciliation, this image is called into question. Certainly, it is unwise to see the confessor as a judge passing sentence on a criminal, yet judgment is nonetheless part of the sacrament. It is helpful to recall that such judgment is, in New Testament language, *diakresis*, or discernment. The confessor helps the penitent judge, or discern, his or her own behavior in light of the Gospel. In confession, the priest may need to ask the penitent questions to clarify issues and avoid vagueness. An important element in this questioning will be "the correction of superficial or distorted ideas of sin."[30] As part of the power of the keys, there may even be times when the confessor withholds absolution. This may occur when no real sin has been confessed, or when there is manifest impenitence. The former case requires discernment and teaching; the latter is possible but unlikely. Given the voluntary nature of Reconciliation in Anglicanism, there is always a *prima facie* assumption of the penitent's sincerity.[31]

The image of the confessor as judge is balanced and enlarged by another ancient image: the confessor as physician. The judgment, or discernment, is thus quite close to the diagnosis and prescription of the physician. Reconciliation is, clearly, a healing sacrament, and the New Testament teaches us to see healing as a matter of the whole person. Francis Belton, in his classic *Manual for Confessors*, calls us to see the analogy between the healing of body and soul. The confessor's work is to diagnose the root sin, of which the penitent's actions are symptomatic, and then prescribe treatment. Appropriate remedies include prayer and meditation, frequent confession, frequent communion, and spiritual reading.[32] As part of spiritual diagnosis, Ross refers to the "healing truth" that temptation is not the same as sin. He goes on to discuss the distinction between mortal and venial sins. While allowing its usefulness to the confessor in assessing proper remedies, Ross suggests that the penitent's attention be directed more to the grace of God than the power of sin, to divine healing rather than to the progress of the disease.[33]

The confessor may also serve as a person's spiritual director and guide. Historically, much spiritual direction has been done in the confessional, and the rubrics clearly suggest that this is not inappropriate. In Form One, for example, after the confession the priest "may offer counsel, direction, and comfort" (*BCP*, p. 447). Anglican commentators suggest that this counsel and direction be kept brief and direct. Extended conversation for guidance is better done outside the confessional, in an informal setting conducive to a much wider consideration of the person's life than just her or his experience of sin. Nonetheless, Reconciliation and spiritual guidance are related to each other, and, as Leech noted in the passage with which we began this section, the same qualities are valuable in both works. A regular confessor needs a sound grounding in ascetical theology and should be thoroughly familiar with the literature of spiritual direction. If the confessor offers any advice, it should be based on a sound knowledge of both theology and psychology. But the essence of sacramental Reconciliation is absolution, not advice.

The other side of the confessor's role as guide is that of fellow-pilgrim with the penitent. There should be a healthy mutuality of

confessor and penitent as both strive against sin and seek to grow
in faithfulness. This can be manifested in many ways, among
them, according to Leech, "It is helpful to pray aloud with the
penitent, to say an act of sorrow together, to say the thanksgiving
or penance together."[35] Further, the commentators unanimously
agree that anyone who regularly ministers Reconciliation should
be regular in the use of the same sacrament. Many quote
approvingly from Dietrich Bonheffer:

> It is not a good thing for one person to be the confessor for all the
> others. All too easily this one person will be overburdened; thus
> confession will become for him an empty routine and this will give
> rise to the disastrous misuse of the confessional for the exercise of
> spiritual domination of souls. In order that he may not succumb to
> this sinister danger of the confessional every person should refrain
> from listening to confession who does not himself practice it. Only
> the person who has so humbled himself can hear a brother's con-
> fession without harm.[36]

A corollary is the established principle that no one should pre-
sume to work as a spiritual guide without being in direction.
"Physician, heal thyself" is a pretty good maxim for most forms of
pastoral practice.

The rich imagery of confessor as celebrant, parent and
friend, judge and physician, guide and fellow-pilgrim, provides us
with more than enough models to use in the working out of our
own particular way of exercising the ministry of Reconciliation.
Each priest who serves as confessor needs to reflect on and appropriate these images in a concrete and personal way. For this reason,
Reconciliation will always be a unique encounter between persons,
in which the Person of Christ will be made known, in ways ever
fresh and often surprising. Such is the nature of grace.

We conclude our consideration of the confessor's ministry
with a few words about the Seal of Confession. The Prayer Book
rubric is quite clear:

> The content of a confession is not normally a matter of subsequent
> discussion. The secrecy of a confession is morally absolute for the
> confessor, and must under no circumstances be broken. (*BCP*,
> p. 446)

This absolute character has a number of implications. Not only must the confessor never repeat anything heard in confession, but he or she may not act on any information gained thereby. In a profound sense, the priest does not "know" anything heard in confession, and indeed, must seek to forget whatever has been heard. It is inappropriate even to state that one has heard a person's confession, and a priest must not allow another to ask any questions about confessions that have been heard. Even with the penitent, the confessor is not free to discuss matters heard in confession, unless the penitent raises the issue and gives permission. Even then, the whole subsequent conversation is to be held under the seal. The seal is also binding on all persons who may, for some reason, have overheard any part of a confession, and on the penitent as well.[37]

The purpose of the seal is obviously to protect the penitent, but it is also to encourage people to make use of the sacrament. Thus, the importance of the seal goes beyond the act of confession itself and extends to the priest's whole ministry. Leech's words are appropriate to ministers in all circumstances:

> Nothing can undermine one's pastoral work so quickly and so permanently as a reputation for breaking confidences. It should be added that a reputation for gossip and undisciplined chatter, *even unconnected with the confessional,* can damage a priest's reputation almost irreparably. If people think you are the kind of person who *might* break the seal of the confessional, they are unlikely to take the risk. Careful discipline of the tongue at all times is therefore a basic requirement in the confessor.[38]

Reconciliation and Christian Development

In the previous section, we explored the pastoral context of Reconciliation in the Anglican tradition by looking at the pastoral task, the reconciling community, and the priest as confessor. We now turn our attention to the human subject of the ministry of Reconciliation, the person who seeks the sacrament. That person has, of course, been in the forefront of all our previous discussion, but here the uniqueness of the penitent and how that uniqueness contributes to his or her experience of sacramental Reconciliation will be considered.

A useful distinction is that between the validity of a sacrament and its efficacy or fuitfulness, which is a means of distinguishing its objective and subjective aspects. The objective nature of the sacraments is a principle well established in Anglican tradition. In this case, if the penitent is baptized, if the priest-confessor has been duly ordained, and if forms established by the Church or in conformity with its tradition are used, then the sacrament is valid. That is, it will do what the Church says it will do—manifest the forgiveness of God. The penitent who has received absolution *is* forgiven, we believe. However, *being* forgiven, or justified, is one thing; *feeling* forgiven, actualizing divine forgiveness in one's life, is another. A perfectly valid sacrament may produce little or no evident effect in the life of the recipient. He or she may not have any real awareness of spiritual renewal as a result of making a confession. As I have had occasion to observe, the real act of faith in this sacrament may not be the confessing of one's sins, or even moving to genuine contrition; it is believing the absolution and living as one forgiven.

If this is true, then we might want to reflect on how pastoral practice can assist in making the sacrament of Reconciliation more fruitful in the lives of Christians. We cannot do this unless we seek to know more about an individual penitent and how people's personal characteristics affect their participation in this action. If Reconciliation is an encounter between persons, and between persons and God, it is likely to be more fruitful if that encounter meets a person where he or she really is, and as the person he or she is. Since it is in the nature of the human creature to grow and develop, then concern for that growth needs to be part of our pastoral strategy in the ministry of Reconciliation. Thus, in this section, I shall dicuss first my hypotheses about the use of a developmental model in ministering Reconciliation, and then seek to apply the particular model developed in the previous chapter.

The Use of Developmental Stages

If human life can be conceived as a journey, then developmental stages can be seen as signposts along the way, telling us where we have been and where we might be going. They must, as we have noted, be used with caution and not be given more weight than they can bear. They may help us find the way, but they are not themselves the way. Like a map, showing us various routes and intersections, a developmental model shows what we need to be looking for at certain points. Such a model may also give us a vocabulary and a methodology for describing our experience so that it becomes more available to us and to others for reflection and decision.

Using the typology with which this chapter began, I suggest that a developmental model will be most helpful when Reconciliation is a part of the Pilgrim's continuing spiritual guidance of direction. It might also be helpful in preparing the Prodigal's confession, and in developing ways of assisting this person in the return "home." If the Perplexed's confession is preceded or followed by counselling, and it might be, then the model is also useful. It will be most valuable, I think, in Reconciliation over time with the same confessor. I do not think it helpful for the confessor to follow the blessing of a person not well known with, "Before your confession, tell me about your life." Thus, the comments I make are specifically intended for the case of the Pilgrim, although I hope they will be useul in the other cases as well.

If a priest has some sense of the road the Pilgrim has traveled, a developmental model may suggest the issues most likely needing attention. Chief among these issues will be the person's images of God, understanding of sin, and style of relationship to others. The model will also help the confessor-guide to interpret the Pilgrim's experiences. This can be of great help, as spiritual experiences are often perplexing and even frightening without interpretation. Since Reconciliation focuses on sin and forgiveness, that will probably be the place to begin. As Leech observes:

> [The priest] must aid the penitent in the formation of conscience and help to free him from legalistic and superficial notions of sin. Sin is not a matter of violating a set of regulations; sin is that which prevents the flowering of man's glory, and delays his progress to perfection.[39]

In a broader sense, this concern has to do with conversion. As noted in Chapter 4, conversion may be parallel to a movement from one stage or pattern of Christian identity to another. In this movement, Reconciliation has an important role to play, but only if the minister has some sense of the direction this transition may take. On the other hand, a developmental model may enable the confessor to be more patient with a penitent by recognizing the validity of his or her experience in the present. If I understand cognitive-developmental theory, I can bear more patiently my two-year-old's constant questions on a trip, "Daddy, when are we going to get there?" My son is just not capable of understanding the meaning of three hours, or a hundred miles, and there's no sense in expecting him to understand.

In *The Forgiveness of Sins*, Tad Guzie and John McIlhon present an interesting developmental model of the experience of sin and the grace of sacramental reconciliation.[40] In the first stage, sin is a sense of uncleanness, being out of line. In anthropological and biblical terms, this is a concern with purity, especially ritual, physical, and sexual purity. The experience of grace is a washing away of stain and a sense of relief that one is back in step. This then evolves into an experience of sin as not living up to an ideal, with the experience of grace being a renewed enthusiasm at being recommitted to the ideal. In the third, and "final" stage, sin is perceived as involving a failure to take responsibility for our humanness, for being who we are. Sin is experienced as more sorrow at our brokenness than as guilt. At this point, then grace becomes fully an experience of reconciliation, with self, others, and God.

Since who we have been deeply affects who we are, any growth must also enable us to come to terms with our past. A developmental theory must have a sense of continuity as well of transition, if it is to help us to achieve a healthy measure of integration. Stanley Hauerwas addresses this concern when he speaks of the formation of "character" as "narrative," and wrestles with our moral responsibility for past actions in which we do not seem to have been "truly ourselves."

> Not to take responsibility for my response is to risk remaining the person who made that kind of response. Philosophically that seems to be a puzzle, for how am I to explain that I must take responsibility for what I did "unknowingly" in order that I can now claim respon-

sibility for what I am and have become. But as puzzling as the philosophical problem is, the moral intelligibility of claiming such an action as mine is just as sure. For retrospectively all my actions tend to appear more like "what happened to me," than what I did. Yet to claim them as mine is a necessary condition for making my current actions my own. Our ability to make our actions our own— that is, to claim them as crucial to our history—even those we regret, turns out to be a necessary condition for having a coherent sense of self—that is, our character.[41]

The proper use of a developmental model will hold these three concerns in dynamic tension: the presence of grace at each place on the way, the call to move and to grow, and the underlying integrity of a person's character and the whole pilgrimage.

Patterns of Growth and Reconciliation

I would like, now, to try to apply the patterns of Christian growth developed in the previous chapter to the ministry of Reconciliation. In this model, I suggested that we grow as Christians from a heteronomous to a conventional identity, then through autonomy to a theonomous pattern. I will concentrate my attention on the middle two patterns because the data and my own pastoral experience suggest that they are the most common among American Christians.

In the heteronomous pattern characteristic of childhood, the self, image of God, and understanding of sin are all fairly undeveloped. We cannot expect any real sense of moral responsibility from persons in this pattern, for they lack a secure identity. Real participation in sacramental Reconciliation is highly suspect. God's grace is ministered through the love of parents and family, membership in the Christian community, and the Eucharist. In most cases, Reconciliation would simply not be appropriate. Kenneth Leech devotes several pages of *Soul Friend* to the confessions of children, and the interested reader can refer to that.[41] The case of the adult who is still in the heteronomous pattern is somewhat more difficult. He or she may claim a "right" to receive the sacrament, and a priest would be ill-advised to refuse. Catechetical instruction, counselling, and possibly psychotherapy, are recommended to assist this person to a higher stage of development in which Reconciliation would be more fruitful. Pastoral care of an adult in this pattern would be aimed at removing the obstacles to a genuine sense of self that can take responsibility for one's actions. Such ministry would need to be gentle and patient to avoid causing such a "little one" to stumble and fall.

The ministry of Reconciliation at the conventional level is doubly problematic. Not only is a conventional pattern of Christianity less than fully adequate to the Gospel, but we must admit that centuries of penitential practice seem to be anchored squarely in this mode. The person in the conventional pattern is capable, to some extent, of recognizing and taking responsibility for her or his actions. However, sin is likely to be conceived primarily in terms of violating the norms of the group—in this case the Church. The locus of control is exterior, and the conventionally religious will find a sense of security in not having to take much responsibility for owning the norms personally. The appeal to authority makes ethics fairly unreflective and rather superficial. Such a person may approach sacramental reconciliation out of a sense of duty, believing that making a confession is one more form of obeying the rules. Nevertheless, the movement from heteronomy to conventionality represents progress, and conventional religion is a vital part of Christian development. However, a person who is much past adolescence and fixed in this pattern will face adult life with insufficient interior resources and in many cases will be hampered by a dangerous rigidity.

At various points in its history, the Church has become corporately fixated in a conventional pattern, especially with respect to sacramental penance. One has only to look over older material used in preparing penitents—Roman Catholic and Anglican alike—to realize how deeply ingrained was a conventionally juridical notion of sin and grace. Most Roman Catholic commentators since Vatican II have wrestled with what Guzie and McIlhon call "the problem of legalism."[43] Pre-confessional meditations on the Ten Commandments or the Seven Deadly Sins reinforce the notion that sin consists of acts violative of God's laws and for which we must offer satisfaction by submitting ourselves to the discipline of the confessional, under penalty of eternal damnation. This is, of course, a caricature, and these approaches are not without truth and validity. However, it is the basic thrust which yields concern. It causes the penitent to see the sin more than the root sinfulness, the awfulness of judgment more than the sovereign love of God.

An Anglican example of this can be found in *St. Augustine's Prayer Book*, first published by the Order of the Holy Cross in 1947, and for many Episcopalians a basic guide to Catholic churchmanship. In its section on the sacrament of Penance, one is bidden to say this prayer before one's self-examination:

> O Holy Spirit, Source of all light, Spirit of wisdom, of understand-
> ing and of knowledge, come to my assistance and enable me to
> make a good confession. Enlighten me, and help me now to know
> my sins as one day I shall be forced to recognize them before thy
> judgment-seat. Bring to my mind the evil which I have done and
> the good which I have neglected. Permit me not to be blinded by
> self-love. Grant me, moreover, heartfelt sorrow for my transgres-
> sions, knowing how deeply they have wounded the loving Heart of
> my Heavenly Father; and help me to make a good confession that
> all stain of guilt may be washed away in the Precious Blood of my
> Saviour Jesus Christ. Amen.[44]

This is followed by an exercise in self-examination based on the Seven Deadly Sins, stated in tones heavy with judgment.[45] The list is theologically unexceptionable, but it is hard to avoid the implication that one earns forgiveness by being just as hard on oneself as possible. The emphasis is less on the formation of conscience and character than on knowing the rules and keeping them.

St. Augustine's Prayer Book is hardly alone in this approach to the Christian life. When the television evangelists of the New Religious Right thunder against sin and immorality, they do so in the same mode. The approach is especially pernicious when the virutes of Christianity are unreflectively equated with a bourgeois celebration of the American Way of Life. Somehow, I question whether this is what Jesus and the New Testament really mean by sin. This is where a large number of contemporary Christians are, however. The pastor's task consists in moving people beyond this view while not scandalizing them into unfaith or antinomianism.

Perhaps one fruitful approach is seen in the questions which Jesus asked his disciples, "But who do *you* say that I am?" In confession and spiritual direction, the priest can push the conventional penitent toward a reflection on *why* the acts confessed are sinful, on the effect the acts have on the person's *relationships*. We might not ask only, "What did you do?" but "What kind of person do you think you are, or are becoming?" As Jesus sought to probe the spirit of the law, so we can ask penitents to seek the deeper meaning of the rules they are conscious of breaking. Further, the attention of a penitent can be re-directed—away from his or her own sins and to the love and grace of God, and the freedom to which he calls his children. In Gilligan's terms, we want to ask not only what is just, fair, and right, but how we can be faithful to the persons for whom we are responsible, including ourselves.

To be pastorally responsible in this endeavor, the priest must recognize the pain of growth and movement. I am struck by how the passage from a conventional Christian identity to an autonomous and theonomous pattern parallels the great biblical movement out of Egypt and into the wilderness. The false security of having all the answers is left behind, and we travel on, with only our faith to sustain us, since we have never seen the Land of Promise toward which we journey. Ministry in this context can be a lonely task. One hopes that the people we ordain are living out at least an autonomous pattern of Christian identity. If so, they are often likely to feel themselves "ahead of" their people. It takes great insight, courage, and patience to be in that place. We must also recognize that it is in the movement from conventionality to autonomy that we first really encounter the hiddenness of God, the mystery of Christian faith. Such a discovery is profoundly unsettling; we may well wish for the fleshpots of Egypt. Somehow, the confessor must be able to meet conventional penitents where they are, affirm the goodness and validity of their faith experience, and yet invite and entice them to move on, sustained by promise.

The ministry of Reconciliation to those moving from a conventional to an autonomous pattern of faith, as well as to those living out the latter pattern, should be prepared to support the questioning and struggling that is a sign of growth. The confessor should seek to help the person discern and clarify what he or she believes in the context of Christian freedom. The penitent may need to hear clearly that God loves him or her and is an active participant in the effort for a deeper personal commitment. There is great value in wrestling with the norms and disciplines of the Christian life; that effort should be blessed. At the same time, the confessor may need to help a person in this pattern focus beyond the merely personal to the corporate and social implications of Christian faith. Interpersonal relationships and action in the world may be the locus of moral decision-making. The black-and-white of earlier ethical sensitivity yields to shades of gray, and a tolerance for ambiguity becomes a positive virtue. Nonetheless, Christian norms need to be articulated clearly so that autonomous faith is not mired down in subjectivity, relativism, and antinomianism.

A great theme for reflection by those in the autonomous pattern, as well as the theonomous pattern, is the sustaining love of God. Penitents can be led not only to concentrate on this love as it is manifested in their own experience, but on the signs of their own response to that love. It is probable that at this stage, we love God better than we know, and the confessor can do much to relieve anxiety. We need to be reassured that in Baptism we have received the Spirit, who is ever present to guide and sustain us in our efforts to be faithful. Sin should be seen as a failure to respond as fully as we can to this presence and as a failure to live fully in relationship with others and with God. The appropriate tone of the pastoral conversation is supportive and encouraging.

A good example of this approach can be seen in a recent publication on *How to Make a Confession*, published by the Order of the Holy Cross, to replace the more conventional tract taken from *St. Augustine's Prayer Book*. The section on self-examination begins:

> If you have decided to make a confession, you have probably already gone a long way towards making a preparation.... Being able to make the decision says a lot about you: it says that you have faith in a God who loves you and who wants to forgive you, who proved that desire for your forgiveness by giving his only Son to die for you; it says that you recognize his love and your falling short of the mark. Most of all, it says you are prepared to begin once again to live the life you received at your Baptism, the life of the Risen Lord Jesus.[46]

After reflecting in silence on the love of God, the penitent is told:

> There is no need to dwell on your sins, you have already repented,

but now you have come to ask the Church's official stamp of absolution, both for quieting your conscience, so that it may not accuse you, and to restore you to the sinlessness and your share in the New Life which God gave you through her at your Baptism. Say a short prayer for yourself, so that you may faithfully recall and confess those things which accuse your conscience, and for the priest who will hear your confession, so that he may give you courage and good advice to help you explore the possibilities of this New Life in Jesus Christ.[48]

"Exploring the possibilities of the New Life in Jesus Christ" is a good watchword for Christian growth through the pattern of autonomy to a theonomous faith.

The pamphlet suggests that after the penitent has reflected on her or his own sense of sins committed, he or she reflect on the Christian virtues of generosity, truth, justice, forgiveness, trust, love, and faith. The emphasis is not on rules broken but on virtues inadequately lived out. The section concludes:

If, by the grace of God, you have managed to avoid all these things, still, remember Jesus' words: "And when you have done all, say, "We are unprofitable servants." For the greatest sin of all is thinking that by our own merits we have pleased God, when the truth is that we are called his sons and daughters only because his eternal Son ever lives to make intercession for us.

It is our task to glory only in the Cross of our Lord Jesus Christ, and to live his Risen Life with joy. Go in peace, then, for the Lord has put away your sin..[48]

Such an approach captures contemporary theological reflection on Reconciliation, rooted in a renewed doctrine of Baptism, and can be very helpful in calling Christians to a greater spiritual maturity.

The developmental literature leads us to assume that people are likely to remain in the autonomous pattern for some time and that the transition to a more theonomous Christian identity is unlikely before mid-life. The ministry of Reconciliation at this stage may be helpful in enabling Christians to come to terms with a sense of defeat and regret at the "roads not taken" in earlier life and to affirm the goodness of what has been. As Hauerwas has suggested, the person moving to theonomous faith will need to see a coherence in her or his character and personal narrative, a coherence characterized by ambiguity and paradox. A central task at this point in life will be to re-appropriate one's own story, link it more explicitly with the Christian story, and release energies, previously expended in forming a self, for a deeper solidarity with the whole created order. The quest for perfection is not abandoned, but a greater acceptance of imperfection, in oneself and others, can lead us from cynicism and despair. As we come to see life more and more a gift, we may need to be forgiven our own refusal to accept gifts, and to share them. As our past is reclaimed, with all its ambiguities, we become more open to the future. Dag Hammarskjöld's words sum up this passage admirably: "For all that has been—thanks! For all that will be—yes!"[48]

My hunch is that the confessor for this person will be primarily a listener and witness to a dialogue between the penitent and God, offering the absolution as an affirmation of the truth that has been discovered. Reconciliation will be more and more a quiet and prayerful attending to the "still, small voice" and a discerning of the path ahead. The minister of Reconciliation may help transmute a heightened sense of morality into a deeper participation in the dying and rising to new life of Jesus, and a more profound involvement in God's re-creation of the world. Thus, participation in the sacrament becomes, for penitent and confessor alike, a contemplative experience of divine love and presence.

Celebrating Reconciliation

Throughout this work, I have intentionally emphasized the theology of Reconciliation and the psychological and spiritual formation of those who celebrate it. I believe that this is the heart of pastoral ministry, against which the details and techniques of performance are minor, though not unimportant. Pastoral practice rooted in good theology and real sensitivity to people can hardly go too wrong. It is useful, however, to consider some of the practicalities involved in preparing people for sacramental reconciliation and in administering the rite. In doing so, I want to continue to focus on the three basic elements: the community and its tradition, the individual who comes for the sacrament, and the priest who ministers it. Anything said here about the administration of Reconciliation should be consistent with good liturgical and pastoral practice for all the sacraments and rituals of the Church's life. Careful preparation and graceful administration go a long way to ensure that what the Church intends is truly manifested in the lives of Christ's people.

Preparing for the Sacrament

Preparing people for Reconciliation has both long-range and immediate aspects and should be aimed both at the community and the individual. Strategically, the long-range and communal preparation is more important and more fruitful. Without it, work with individuals is likely to be largely remedial and risks being superficial. A proper celebration of Reconciliation derives from who we are as community, individual, and priest, and this is the proper concern of formation, nurture, and catechesis.

Catechetical instruction, in the broadest sense, is the foundation of all pastoral practice. It is vitally important that the People of God know who they are, how God is calling them to new life, what this means for them. Since the great sacrament of Christian identity is Baptism, with its regular *anamnesis* in the Eucharist, this is the place to start. Christian formation should aim at enabling people to live out their baptism, and there are many encouraging signs of a renewal of baptismal teaching in the Episcopal Church.[50] Since Reconciliation is a renewal of our Baptism, an appreciation for the one will enhance the understanding of the other. The work of John Westerhoff and others gives a number of good models for forming the life of a Christian community that can nurture its members in the norms and actions of Christian life. There has also been a flowering of community-oriented Christian education and practice in the Roman Catholic Church since Vatican II, much of it directly relevant to Reconciliation.[51]

The present recovery of concern for spiritual direction also provides abundant resources to help prepare people for Reconciliation. Programs of individual and group spiritual guidance should include a serious consideration of sin and forgiveness, which may orient people toward sacramental Reconciliation. There is likewise a greater interest in spiritual healing, and Reconciliation is a healing sacrament. Teaching about the rite and its meaning will naturally accompany a consideration of healing. The practice of sacramental confession may also be the result of a deepened commitment to the Christian life, flowing from the various renewal movements in today's Church. This is the pastoral context of which Reconciliation is a part.

In a time of rapid change, rampant injustice, ethical nihilism, and the threat of nuclear and ecological catastrophe, it is imperative that the Church become what Browning calls a "community of moral discourse." Practical ways of relating Christian doctrine to the personal, social, political, and economic issues of contemporary life are sorely needed. Such a concern may take many forms, from large conferences on a particular issue, to case-study groups, to vigorous discussions in the adult education program. People are perplexed and seek guidance in acting as faithful Christians in a troubled world. This, too, is part of the context of the Church's total ministry of reconciliation, of which the sacrament is a sign and means.

The Good News of forgiveness is an integral part of the Church's liturgical life, and our conscience is formed by confronting both the ethical demands of the Gospel and God's promise of forgiveness as we worship. While a concern with sin and grace is always present in the liturgy, on certain occasions and in certain seasons it is especially prominent. Historically, Advent and Lent have been considered times when we are called to face our betrayal of God's gifts, to repent and return. Penitential services, with appropriate preaching, at such times helps form the community that celebrates Reconciliation. It is undoubtedly for this reason that so many Roman Catholic commentators have called for the use of corporate services of penance as part of the renewal of individual Reconciliation in the new *Rite of Penance. The Book of Common Prayer* provides substantial material for such a service, especially in the Penitential Orders preceding the Eucharist (*BCP*, pp. 319–21, 351–53) and the Ash Wednesday Liturgy (*BCP*, pp. 264–69).

Finally, adequate long-range preparation for Reconciliation

needs to be done through specific teaching, at various times and in various ways. Probably many Episcopalians do not even know about The Reconciliation of a Penitent; or, if they know it exists, they do not understand it. And how are they to understand if it is not explained, and how is it to be explained unless their clergy and other leaders take the time to do it? In older Anglo-Catholic practice, priests were urged to "preach the confessional," and this notion is not entirely obsolete. The theology of Reconciliation can be the stuff of which edifying sermons are made, an opportunity to proclaim the Good News with conviction and a very concrete way to do something about it. In preparing people for Confirmation and Reception, a clear statement of the Anglican practice of sacramental confession would be helpful to many. Since Baptism is increasingly a public and corporate act, no longer hidden off in a corner on Sunday afternoon, it might be an appropriate time to let Reconciliation "come out of the closet" as a significant pastoral ministry. The practice of having stated times when confessions are heard, with this noted in the Sunday bulletin and parish newsletter, may stimulate some interest, and show that at least the priest thinks this is important. Kenneth Ross ocmmends this practice:

> Many times . . . there will be no one to avail himself of [the priest's] ministrations, but at the least he will have some time for the refreshment of his own soul and for the meditation and spiritual reading that otherwise get crowded out of a busy life. And one never knows who will turn up, to whom one's priestly ministrations will be of untold value.[52]

A course or teaching mission on repentance and renewal might also help people come to a better understanding of the rite and be more disposed to use it.

Like it or not, the clergy tend to serve as role models for the Christian community, and so their own attention to spiritual growth will have an effect. I assume that being "a wholesome example to one's people" will include an intentional spiritual life, regular consultation with a spiritual guide or confessor, and continued study of ascetical and moral theology and ethics. These serve as the priest's long-range preparation for the ministry of Reconciliation, as well as forming a fruitful pastoral identity.

Besides forming the priest as a faithful pastor and confessor, these practices demonstrate to the people that such things are important.

How, then, are the individual members of the Christian community best prepared to receive the sacrament of Reconciliation? Fr. Ross suggests that special efforts are appropriate for one about to make a first confession. The priest should meet the neophyte penitent before the latter makes a confession, so that the sacrament is fully understood. Questions can be asked, assurance given, and some of the awkwardness dispelled. Ross suggests, by the way, that it be made clear that the would-be penitent is not obliged to come to the Rector for confession, but may go to any priest. Indeed, the priest might want to suggest a few in the vicinity. Some people will find making a confession to their own priest unbearably threatening. When the penitent decides to come for the sacrament, Ross also suggests that it be done by appointment the first time so that there will be plenty of time for walking slowly through the procedure, that any embarrassment can be minimized.[53]

How people prepare for their confessions will be a very individual matter. A certain experimentation should be encouraged until one finds the most helpful way. Some general rules hold, nonetheless. The person should find a quiet time and place and begin with centering prayer. This is a prayer for illumination; the penitent asks the Holy Spirit to show the ways he or she has failed to be faithful. Meditation on Scripture is often a good beginning. The Scriptures may be opened at random, or certain particular passages selected. Fr. Ross suggests the Beatitudes, Romans 12:8–14, 1 Corinthians 13, and Galatians 5:13–26.[54] Confrontation with the Word in silence opens our hearts and minds to an encounter with God. As Guzie and McIlhon observe, "Quiet, silence and stillness are the best atmosphere we can create for hearing God's invitation."[55]

Most modern writers suggest that we frame our confession in positive terms, that is, by recognizing how we have failed to live up to God's love, rather than which rules we have broken. A self-examination using a "sin list" may not be very helpful. If it is used at all, it should probably follow one's own reflections, to see if there is any area of sin we are avoiding. We need to meditate on the direction of our lives, on the basic sinfulness our actions manifest, more than on the actions themselves. At the same time, we need to be concrete, because we fail God, neighbor, and self in concrete and specific ways. Charles Curran, noted Roman Catholic moral theologian, suggests a self-examination based on our relationships to God, neighbor, self, and the world, adding:

> From looking at *acts*, our examen should proceed to a searching look at *self*, to discover there the lack of harmony and peace, the pockets of violence, selfishness, stiff-necked pride, and vindic- tiveness. This, then, should lead to a genuine expression of *regret*, a desire of conversion, a determination to set things right.[56]

Most people find it helpful to write down the results of their self- examination. This is not only a useful aid to making the con- fession, but the destruction of the list after the absolution can be a powerful sign that one believes that God has put away one's sins.

When the penitent comes for confession, he or she should spend some time in silent prayer and preparation, probably in the Church. The confessor, too, needs preparation, especially if sev- eral confessions are to be heard. Ministering Reconciliation is hard work if it is done well, as intense concentration is required. The confessor should be rested, quieted, and prepared by silent prayer or meditation. Indeed, the whole atmosphere of the sacra- ment should be peaceful and prayerful. When confessor and penitent are centered and prepared, they meet at the place of confession.

That place can be one of several possible arrangements. The rubrics of *The Book of Common Prayer* state:

> When a confession is heard in a church building, the confessor may sit inside the altar rails or in a place set aside to give greater privacy, and the penitent kneels nearby. If preferred, the confessor and penitent may sit face to face for a spiritual conference leading to absolution or a declaration of forgiveness. (*BCP*, p. 446)

The normal Anglican practice is to hear confessions at the altar rail, with the confessor in a chair facing the altar and the penitent kneeling at the rail. Kenneth Ross urges that all confessions be heard in the church, unless there is weighty cause, so that the

proper tone can be achieved, and his view has much to recom-
mend it.[57] It may be helpful to use a side chapel, or some other
more intimate and protected space, if there be such.

Some churches do have confessional booths, or "boxes,"
known also to generations of irreverent seminarians as "sin bins."
These do provide privacy, but are almost claustrophobic and tend
to inhibit the sense of pastoral warmth and mutuality that all the
contemporary rites commend. Further, it makes the laying-on of
hands impossible, and any other manual gesture invisible. The
Roman Catholic Church has largely abandoned confessional
booths in favor of "reconciliation rooms." These spaces provide a
kneeler behind a grill at the entrance for those who still prefer
anonymous confessions, but also add a space beyond for face-to-
face conversation. I doubt that too many Anglican churches will
go to the effort and expense of such a room, but the same effect
can be achieved in the priest's study or some other quiet corner of
the church building.

Whatever the space, two primary considerations need to be
kept in mind. First, the space should be conducive to the devotional aspects of the rite. The penitent should probably face a
cross, crucifix, icon, or some other vivid symbol of the Gospel. If
held in a room other than the church, care needs to be taken to
remind the participants that this is a celebration of a sacrament,
not a little chat with the Rector. The second and obvious consideration is privacy. The hearing of confessions should be so
arranged that there is no chance of anyone overhearing it, or even
noticing who is making a confession, how long it takes, or what the
priest does. In my own parish, a few steps away from the church,
there is a chapel in which the Sacrament is reserved. It provides an
appropriate space for hearing confessions, out of the way of other
people. It is not very helpful to celebrate Reconciliation while the
Altar Guild is bustling around, setting up for Sunday.

Anglican pastoral tradition suggests flexibility and experimentation in the matter of arrangements. I have made confessions
in a wide variety of settings, from sitting cross-legged on the lawn
in front of a monastery chapel, to a very tight little confessional.
Personally, I prefer to sit facing the priest in a study or church,
kneeling to receive the absolution and laying-on of hands.

Orthodox practice even suggests the possibility of confessor and penitent standing together, facing an icon. The best arrangement is that best for the penitent and most conducive to his or her wholehearted participation. Whatever the physical arrangements, the tone should be peaceful, prayerful, supportive and encouraging. We are ministering the Good News of God's forgiveness, not passing sentence on some wretch in the dock!

Dennis Michno, in *A Priest's Handbook*, makes some helpful suggestions about the ceremonial of this rite. The celebrant is normally vested in cassock and surplice or alb, with a stole, usually purple. Even if the confessor is not vested, the stole is a reminder that the priest is exercising a ministry on behalf of the Church, and not just performing a personal service. At the initial blessing, the priest may make the sign of the cross over the penitent. At the absolution, the priest may extend a hand over the penitent, make the sign of the cross, lay hands on the penitent's head, or place the stole over the penitent's shoulder.[58] Following the dismissal, it is quite appropriate for the confessor and penitent to exchange the Peace, with a handshake or embrace.

During the confession, the priest listens attentively and may ask questions to clarify the issues raised. As observed above, these should be brief and to the point. The priest should allow the penitent plenty of time and not worry about long pauses. Since both forms in the Prayer Book provide further words after the confession itself, it should not be too difficult to determine when the penitent has finished. Then, as the rubrics note,

> When the penitent has confesseed all serious sins troubling the conscience and has given evidence of due contrition, the priest gives such counsel and encouragement as are needed and pronounces the absolution. Before giving absolution, the priest may assign to the penitent a psalm, prayer, or hymn to be said, or something to be done, as a sign of penitence and act of thanksgiving. (*BCP*, p. 446)

This is technically called "the penance." In Anglican practice it is optional and not understood as integral to the sacrament. The penance is, rather, a way of expressing the penitent's response in a meaningful way. The real art of assigning helpful penances probably needs to be worked out in each priest's own practice. Ross makes some useful suggestions. He regards the penance as a token of new life and something "medicinal," that is, chosen for its appropriateness to the penitent's condition. No public penance can be given for a secret sin, and if some action is given, it must be one that will respect the seal of the confession. An act of devotion may be recommended, but it should be made clear that this is not itself the penance.[59]

The penance should be relevant to the needs of the penitent, but should be neither so complicated nor so vague that it cannot be carried out. At the same time, it should not be trivial or too easy. An example of both can be seen in a story told by the late Canon Colin Stephenson. As a young man, he was given a penance, "Go and make yourself a living sacrifice." He worried about this for some time until another priest told him, "Don't worry about it, say three Hail Marys."[60] The priest may commend making some form of restitution to those wronged, but again, this should be readily done and not create further difficulties or open new wounds. Guzie and McIlhon offer sound advice on this score:

> A penance ought not to carry with it a note of finality. Rather, it is like a baton in a relay race.... Penance means renewal and that process never ends.[61]

After the absolution, dismissal (and Peace), the penitent should return to the church or some other quiet place. Here the penance can be performed, if it is a prayer, psalm, or hymn, and some time can be spent in prayer, reflecting on the new life one has been called to lead and giving thanks to God for the great grace of the sacrament. The confessor, too, should conclude the celebration of Reconciliation with prayerful intercession for those whose confessions have been heard. In the prayer, it is appropriate to give thanks for God's mercy and to offer up the penitent(s) to God's keeping and love. Max Thurian comments regarding the seal;

> In his prayers [the confessor] must ask God to grant that these things be blotted out from his memory. The confessor must pray God that the absolution which he addresses to the penitent may act not only upon the spiritual state of the latter, but also be equally effective on his own mind.[62]

The celebration of Reconciliation should end as it began, with prayer, awe, and joy and the wonderful love of God, who in Christ has put away all our sins, all obstacles to our relationship with him, and reconciled us, restoring to us the gracious liberty of the Sons and Daughters of God.

VI

The Priestly Ministry
of Reconciliation

THE Christian life is life lived no longer under sin and death, but life lived in the light of God's grace. As the Catechism reminds us,

> Grace is God's favor towards us, unearned and undeserved; by grace God forgives our sins, enlightens our minds, stirs our hearts, and strengthens our wills. (*BCP*, p. 858)

In a fallen world, it is not easy to live under grace and we need to be reminded constantly who we are and how we are called to live. The sacraments are Christ's special gifts to his people, by which we are reformed, renewed, and recalled to our identity and mission in the world. In each sacrament, the Gospel is proclaimed in its fullness and manifested in the life of the Christian community. It has been my purpose in this study to show how this occurs through the sacramentality of Reconciliation, and it is appropriate, in conclusion, to summarize what we have discovered.

In our historical review of the development of sacramental reconciliation we can discern a kind of creative tension along two polarities, out of which the Church's understanding and practice has been formed. Renewal has tended to occur when one end of the polarity has been recovered. These poles are formed by the tensions between the community and the individual, on one axis, and between a rigorist approach and a more pastoral approach on the other. There is a continual need for the Christian community to assert its integrity and call people to the demanding standards of the Gospel on the one hand, and yet there is an equal need to deal gracefully with weak and fallible human beings on the other. The Church's aim is to assist its members in being faithful to their Baptism, which has both corporate and individual aspects. In the Anglican tradition, the emphasis has been on the pastoral and voluntary character of Reconciliation, which respects the freedom of the individual Christian yet calls him or her to be accountable to the whole Body of Christ and its mission.

In examining contemporary rites of sacramental reconciliation, the degree of ecumenical consensus is striking. God is calling his Church to a greater degree of unity, and I believe that Reconciliation is a signal instance of this call. In all the rites, we find a heightened pastoral sensitivity, a greater awareness of the corporate and social aspects of Reconciliation, and a concern for the conversion of the faithful as a life-long process. It is God's will that Christians be formed both as individuals capable of acting under grace and as a community capable of making that grace known in the world.

The concern for Christian nurture and formation leads us to seek out resources in a variety of places including the "secular" human sciences. Indeed, we are called to recover a more holistic view of the human creation to transcend the false dichotomy of sacred and secular. The human person is not just a collection of cognitive functions, ego strengths, or prosocial behaviors, but all of these, and more. We are spiritual creatures, the sum of emotion, intellect, intuition, sensation and will, given life by the very Spirit of God. Under the leading of that Spirit, we grow in our capacity to life faithfully. As we grow, we become more distinctively the people we are, and yet also more and more able to give ourselves to others. As we grow in faith, we affirm more and more the paradox of Christian life, that by losing ourselves in Christ, we find ourselves. In this growth, we are increasingly reconciled to ourselves, to our neighbors, and to God.

Such a holistic understanding needs also to inform the pastoral practice of the Christian Church. Authentic pastoral ministry is the bringing together of a clear theological understanding of the task, a concern for the life of the community as a focus of moral discourse, Christian formation and faithful action, attention to the work and qualities of the community's representative minister, and the ability to encounter the individual in her or his uniqueness. Sacramental reconciliation is a powerful means by which the Church fulfills this task in the lives of its members.

I contend that this task will be greatly aided by a renewal of pastoral theology in the life of the Church. If I have succeeded in my aim, this study can serve as an example of how pastoral theology can meet our need for informed ministry in the present context. Sound pastoral theology can synthesize resources from such diverse disciplines as history, liturgics, ascetical theology, psychology and the other social sciences, and then suggest ways these resources can be applied in concrete and particular situations. All too often we have concentrated either on the historical-theoretical dimension or the practical-technical without seeking to bring them all together. This approach risks either a disembodied erudition or an unreflective obsession with methods and techniques. As Christians are called to being and action, so pastoral theology is, I believe, called to a holistic concern with theory and practice, each informed by the other. We need, in a sense, to be able to answer all those journalistic questions: what to do and why, as well as how, when, where, and with whom.

Our goal, in all of this, is to actualize the priestly ministry of Christ in this world. Christ is, as Hebrews so eloquently testifies, our great High Priest, our intercessor and mediator, the proclaimer of the Good News of Redemption, and the means by whom that redemption is accomplished. Through his Spirit, Christ has conferred that priesthood to his Body, the priestly people, the Church. As the context of Christ's priestly ministry is the whole world, so is the world the context of the priesthood of all Christians. That world, which is fallen and yet redeemed, needs to be convicted of sin, called to repentance, and assured of the forgiving love of its creator. Christ's call is always, "Repent and believe the Good News." His call comes again and again to us who bear his name, and we extend that call to all our brothers and sisters in that name.

The call of Christ is never only a general call; it comes with a demand for decision and response to each and every person in concrete and particular ways. The sacrament of Reconciliation comprehends both the universal and the particular and is a sacramental manifestation, a focused example, an *anamnesis* of the whole to the individual. In it, priest and penitent act both as individuals and yet as representatives. The priest represents the whole priestly people and, by ordination, Christ himself. The penitent represents every sinner on the way to salvation, dying to sin and rising again in Christ. Yet priest and penitent are both sinners *and* members of the redeemed community. Their participation in the sacrament makes present the Good News in the here and now, and also is part of the whole history of creation, redemption, and sanctification, which is the cosmic drama of God's love for those whom he has made.

Whenever the sacrament of Reconciliation is celebrated, there is a powerful proclamation of the love that overcomes sin, separation, meaninglessness, and death. This is indeed the Good News the world longs to hear. By faithful and informed participation in this sacramental act, we cooperate with God's loving intention for all humankind.

> From now on, therefore, we regard no one from a human point of view; even though we once regarded Chirst from a human point of view, we regard him thus no longer. Therefore, if anyone is in Christ, he is a new creation; the old has passed away, behold, the new has come. All this is from God, who through Christ reconciled us to himself and gave us the ministry of reconciliation; that is, in Christ God was reconciling the world to himself, not counting their trespasses against them, and entrusting to us the message of reconciliation. So we are ambassadors for Christ, God making his appeal through us. We beseech you on behalf of Christ, be reconciled to God. For our sake he made him to be sin who knew no sin, so that in him we might become the righteousness of God. (2 Corinthians 5:16-21)

Appendix A: Luther on "The Office of the Keys and Confession"

What is the office of the keys?
It is the special power which Christ has given to his church on earth to forgive the sins of repentant sinners, but to retain the sins of the impenitent as long as they do not repent.

Where is this written?
Our Lord Jesus Christ said to Peter in the sixteenth chapter of Matthew: "I will give you the keys of the kingdom of heaven, and whatever you bind on earth shall be bound in heaven, and whatever you loose on earth shall be loosed in heaven."
He said the same to his disciples in the twentieth chapter of John: "Receive the Holy Spirit. If you forgive the sins of any, they are forgiven; of you retain the sins of any, they are retained."

What is confession?
Confession consists of two parts: the one is that we confess our sins; the other that we receive absolution or forgiveness through the confessor, as from God himself, in no wise doubting, but firmly believing that our sins are thus forgiven before God in heaven.

What sins should we confess?
In the presence of God we should acknowledge ourselves guilty of all sins, even those which we do not know, as we do in the Lord's Prayer. But in the presence of the confessor we should confess only those sins which we know and feel in our hearts.

Which are these?
Here look at your station in the light of the Ten Commandments, whether you are a father, mother, son, or daughter, in whatever vocation and service you may be, and consider whether you have been disobedient, unfaithful, wrathful, unchaste, quarrelsome, whether you have hurt anyone by words or actions, whether you have stolen or neglected anything or done any other evil.

How do you confess your sins in the presence of the confessor?
You may say to the confessor: "I ask you to hear my confession and assure me of forgiveness for God's sake." Then confess yourself guilty to all sins before God, and in the presence of the confessor confess whatever particular sins or offenses lie heavy upon you.
You may conclude your confession with these words: "For all this I am sorry. I plead for grace. I will amend my ways."

How is the absolution given?

The confessor says: "God be gracious to you and strengthen your faith. Amen. Do you believe that my forgiveness is also God's forgiveness?" Answer: "Yes, this I believe." Thereupon he says: "As you believe, so be it done to you. And I, in obedience to the command of our Lord Jesus Christ, do forgive you sins in the name of the Father, and of the Son, and of the Holy Ghost. Amen. Go in peace!"

But those whose conscience is heavily burdened or who are distressed and tempted a father confessor will know how to comfort and stir up to faith with further words from Holy Scripture.

Source: Herbert Girgensohn, *Teaching Luther's Catechism*, Volume II (see chap. 3, n. 37), pp. 62–63.

Appendix B: Structure of the Rites of Reconciliation

Book of Common Prayer Form I, pp. 447–48	Book of Common Prayer Form II, pp. 449–51	Rite of Penance 1974 pp. 32ff.	Lutheran Book of Worship pp. 322–23
Reception of the Penitent Blessing	Reception of the Penitent Psalm 51 Blessing	Reception of the Penitent Greeting Sign of the Cross Invitation to Trust in God	Reception of the Penitent Greeting Psalm 51
	Reading of Scripture "Comfortable Words"	Reading of the Word of God	
Confession	Confession Bidding by priest Confession by penitent	Confession of Sins and Acceptance of Satisfaction	Confession
Counsel, Direction, and Comfort	Comfort and Counsel Questions about repentance and forgiveness		Pastoral Conversation and Comfort from the Scriptures
Absolution	Absolution, with the Laying-on of Hands	Prayer of the Penitent and Absolution	Absolution Recitation of Psalm 51 Question about trust in the absolution Absolution, with the Laying-on of Hands
Dismissal of the penitent	Dismissal of the Penitent	Proclamation of Praise of God and Dismissal	Prayer from Psalm 103 Dismissal and The Peace

Appendix C: Erikson's Epigenetic Psychosexual Stages

Stage	Developmental Crisis	Ego Quality that Denotes Successful Development
Oral-Sensory	Basic trust v. mistrust	Hope: The enduring belief in the attainability of fervent wishes
Muscular-anal	Autonomy v. shame and self-doubt	Will power: The unbroken determination to exercise free choice as well as self-restraint
Locomotor-genital	Initiative v. guilt	Purpose: The courage to envisage and pursue valued goals, uninhibited by guilt or the fear of punishment
Latency	Industry v. inferiority	Competence: The free exercise of dexterity and intelligence in the completion of tasks, unimpaired by infantile inferiority
Adolescence	Identity v. role confusion (identity confusion)	Fidelity: The ability to sustain freely pledged loyalties, despite the inevitable contradictions of value systems
Young Adulthood	Intimacy v. isolation	Love: The mutuality of devotion, which subdues the antagonisms inherent in divided functioning
Adulthood	Generativity v. stagnation	Care: The widening concern for others, overcoming the ambivalence to obligations
Maturity	Ego identity v. despair	Wisdom: The detached concern with life in the face of death

Notes
1. *Epigenetic* means "upon emergence," or unfolding through successive differentiation according to an innate schedule.
2. Both the positive and negative characteristics of any stage (e.g., basic trust and mistrust) are present to some degree in every personality. A preponderance of the former denotes healthy adjustment, and results in the emergence of the corresponding ego quality.
3. A favorable or unfavorable resolution of each crisis is by no means permanent, but remains subject to future benign and pathogenic conditions. However, a given ego quality is unlikely to appear unless the preceding stages have developed satisfactorily.

Source: Robert B. Ewen, *An Introduction to Theories of Personality* (see chap. 4, n. 23), p. 231.

Appendix D: Kohlberg's Stages of Moral Development

Level and Stage	Content of Stage		Sociomoral Perspective of Stage
	What Is Right	Reasons for Doing Right	
Level 1: Preconventional: Stage 1. Heteronomous morality	To avoid breaking rules backed by punishment, obedience for its own sake, and avoiding physical damage to persons and property.	Avoidance of punishment and the superior power of authorities.	Egocentric point of view. Doesn't consider the interests of others or recognize that they differ from the actor's, doesn't relate two points of view. Actions are considered physically rather than in terms of psychological interests of others. Confusion of authority's perspective with one's own.
Stage 2. Individualism, instrumental purpose, and exchange	Following rules only when it is to someone's immediate interest; acting to meet one's own interests and needs and letting others do the same. Right is also what's fair, what's an equal exchange, a deal, an agreement.	To serve one's own needs or interests in a world where you have to recognize that other people have their interests, too.	Concrete individualistic perspective. Aware that everybody has his own interests to pursue and these conflict, so that right is relative (in the concrete individualistic sense).
Level 2: Conventional: Stage 3. Mutual interpersonal expectations, relationships, and interpersonal conformity	Living up to what is expected by people close to you or what people generally expect of people in your role as son, brother, friend, etc. "Being good" is important and means having good motives, showing concern about others. It also means keeping mutual relationships, such as trust, loyalty, respect, and gratitude.	The need to be a good person in your own eyes and those of others. Belief in the Golden Rule. Desire to maintain rules and authority which support stereotypical good behavior.	Perspective of the individual in relationships with other individuals. Aware of shared feelings, agreements, and expectations which take primacy over individual interests. Relates points of view through the concrete Golden Rule, putting yourself in the other guy's shoes. Does not yet consider generalized system perspective.

(continued overleaf)

Level and Stage	Content of Stage		Sociomoral Perspective of Stage
	What Is Right	Reasons for Doing Right	
Stage 4. Social system and conscience	Fulfilling the actual duties to which you have agreed. Laws are to be upheld except in extreme cases where they conflict with other fixed social duties. Right is also contributing to society, the group, or institution.	To keep the institution going as a whole, to avoid the breakdown in the system "if everyone did it," or the imperative of conscience to meet one's defined obligations.	Differentiates societal point of view from interpersonal agreement or motives. Takes the point of view of the system that defines roles and rules. Considers individual relations in terms of place in the system.
Level 3: Postconventional, or principled: Stage 5. Social contract or utility and individual rights	Being aware that people hold a variety of values and opinions, that most values and rules are relative to your group. These relative rules should usually be upheld, however, in the interest of impartiality and because they are the social contract. Some nonrelative values and rights like life and liberty, however, must be upheld in any society and regardless of majority opinion.	A sense of obligation to law because of one's social contract to make and abide by laws for the welfare of all and for the protection of all people's rights. A feeling of contractual commitment, freely entered upon, to family, friendship, trust and work obligations. Concern that laws and duties be based on rational calculation of overall utility, "the greatest good for the greatest number."	Prior-to-society perspective. Perspective of a rational individual aware of values and rights prior to social attachments and contracts. Integrates perspectives by formal mechanisms of agreement, contract, objective impartiality, and due process. Considers moral and legal points of view; recognizes that they sometimes conflict and finds it difficult to integrate them.
Stage 6. Universal ethical principles	Following self-chosen ethical principles. Particular laws or social agreements are usually valid because they rest on such principles. When laws violate these principles, one acts in accordance with the principle. Principles are universal principles of justice: the equality of human rights and respect for the dignity of human beings as individual persons.	The belief as a rational person in the validity of universal moral principles, and a sense of personal commitment to them.	Perspective of a moral point of view from which social arrangements derive. Perspective is that of any rational individual recognizing the nature of morality or the fact that persons are ends in themselves and must be treated as such.

Source: Anne Colby et al., *A Longitudinal Study of Moral Judgment* (see chap. 4, n. 31), pp. 3–4.

Appendix E: Eisenberg's Stages of Prosocial Moral Reasoning

Stage 1: Two uncorrelated types of reasoning are grouped together because both are frequently verbalized by the youngest subjects:

Hedonistic, pragmatic orientation: The individual is concerned with selfish or pragmatic consequences rather than moral constructions. "Right" behavior is that which is instrumental for satisfying the actor's own needs or wants. Reasons for assisting or not assisting another include consideration of direct gain to the self, future reciprocity, and concern for others whom the individual needs and/or likes.

"Needs of others" orientation: The individual expresses concern for the physical, material and psychological needs of others even though others' needs conflict with one's own needs. This concern is expressed in the simplest terms, without clear evidence of role taking, verbal expressions of sympathy, or reference to internalized effect such as guilt ("he's hungry" or "she needs it").

Stage 2: Approval and interpersonal orientation and/or sterotyped orientation
Stereotyped images of good and bad persons and behaviors and/or considerations of other's approval and acceptance are used in justifying prosocial or non-helping behaviors. For example, one helps because "it's nice to help" or because "he'd like me more if I helped."

Stage 3a: Empathic orientation
The individual's judgments include evidence of sympathetic responding, role taking, concern with other's humanness, and/or guilt or positive effect related to the consequences of one's actions. Examples include "I know how he feels," "I care about people," and "I'd feel bad if I didn't help him because he'd be in pain."

Stage 3b: Transitional stage
Justifications for helping or not helping involve internalized values, norms, duties, or responsibilities, or refer to the necessity of protecting the rights and dignity of other persons; these ideas, however, are not clearly and strongly stated. References to internalized effect, self-respect and living up to one's own values are considered indicative of this stage if they are weakly stated. Examples include "It's just something I've learned and felt."

Stage 4: Strongly internalized stage

Justification for helping or not helping are based on internalized values, norms, or responsibilities, the desire to maintain individual and societal contractual obligations, the belief in the dignity, rights, and equality of all individuals. Positive or negative effects related to the maintenance of self-respect and living up to one's own values and accepted norms also characterize this stage. Examples of stage 4 reasoning include, "I feel I have a responsibility to help other people in need," or "I would feel bad if I didn't help because I'd know that I didn't live up to my values."

Source: Paul Mussen and Nancy Eisenberg-Berg, *Roots of Caring, Sharing and Helping* (see chap. 4, n. 21), pp. 122–23.

Appendix F: Stages of Human Development: Optimal Parallels

Eras and Ages	Erikson	Piaget	Kohlberg	Fowler
Infancy (0–1½)	Basic Trust v. Mistrust (Hope)	Sensorimotor	—	Undifferentiated Faith
Early Childhood (2–6)	Autonomy v. Shame and Doubt (Will)	Preoperational		1. Intuitive-Projective Faith
	Initiative v. Guilt (Purpose)		Preconventional Level 1. Heteronomous Morality	
Childhood (7–12)	Industry v. Inferiority (Competence)	Concrete Operational	2. Instrumental Exchange	2. Mythic-Literal Faith
Adolescence (13–21)	Identity v. Role Confusion (Fidelity)	Formal Operational	Conventional Level 3. Mutual Interpersonal Relations	3. Synthetic-Conventional Faith
Young Adulthood (21–35)	Intimacy v. Isolation (Love)	—	4. Social System and Conscience	4. Individuative-Reflective Faith
Adulthood (35–60)	Generativity v. Stagnation (Care)	—	Postconventional Principled Level 5. Social Contract, Individual Rights	5. Conjunctive Faith
Maturity (60–)	Integrity v. Despair (Wisdom)	—	6. Universal Ethical Principles	6. Universalizing Faith

Source: James W. Fowler, *Stages of Faith* (see chap. 4, n. 27), pp. 52, 113.

Notes

Chapter II. Reconciliation in History

1. B. Poschmann, *Penance and the Anointing of the Sick* (New York: Herder and Herder, 1964), p. 3.

2. J. A. T. Gunstone, *The Liturgy of Penance* (New York: Morehouse-Barlow, 1966), p. 10.

3. Wllliam Telfer, *The Forgiveness of Sins* (Philadelphia: Muhlenberg Press, 1960), p. 19.

4. Ibid, p. 31.

5. For a fuller treatment of this theme, see Poschmann, pp. 9–12.

6. Kenneth Ross, *Hearing Confessions* (London: SPCK, 1974), 10.

7. See Poschmann, pp. 20–25, and Gunstone, pp. 17–25.

8. Telfer, p. 60.

9. Ibid, pp. 62–72; Poschmann, pp. 35–79. Other extended accounts of this development can be found in R. C. Mortimer, *The Origins of Private Penance in the Western Church* (Oxford: The Clarendon Press, 1939), chap. 2, and Karl Rahner, *Penance in the Early Church*, vol. 15 of *Theological Investigations*, trans. Lionel Swain (New York: Crossroads, 1982).

10. Gunstone, pp. 31–39; Poschmann, pp. 82–86.

11. Poschmann, pp. 88–96.

12. Telfer, pp. 86–91.

13. Poschmann, pp. 114–21; Ross, pp. 11–12.

14. Gunstone, p. 44.

15. Mortimer, p. 3. Augustine and the Council of Toledo, respectively, are quoted.

16. John T. McNeill, *A History of the Cure of Souls* (New York: Harper and Row, 1951), p. 115.

17. Poschmann, pp. 124–30.

18. *English Penitential Discipline and Anglo-Saxon Law in their Joint Influence* (Columbia University Studies in the Social Sciences, no. 242 (n.p., 1923; reprint, New York: AMS Press, 1969), p. 199.

19. Mortimer, p. 189.

20. Gunstone, p. 53.

21. Ibid., pp. 54–58; Poschmann, pp. 156–67.

22. Poschmann, p. 178.

23. This whole subject is exhaustively covered by Thomas N. Tentler in *Sin and Confession on the Eve of the Reformation* (Princeton, N.J.: Princeton University Press, 1977).

24. Telfer, pp. 107–14; McNeill, pp. 163–70.

25. Telfer, p. 116.

26. Ibid., pp. 128–30; McNeill, pp. 192–217.

27. Poschmann, pp. 197–202.

28. Gunstone, pp. 64–65.

29. Ibid, pp. 71–72; Telfer, pp. 131–32. For making the actual comparisons, an invaluable resource is F. E. Brightman, *The English Rite*, 2 vols. (London: Rivingtons, 1915).

30. Brightman, p. 131.

31. Ibid, pp. 681–83, 698.

32. Ibid., pp. 828–29.

33. Quoted in Marion J. Hachett, *Commentary on the American Prayer Book* (New York: Seabury Press, 1980), pp. 450–51, which contians an excellent summary of the foregoing historical material.

34. Brightman, p. 886. The same exhortation, with only minor revisions, was carried through 1552 and into 1662.

35. Gunstone, pp. 66–69.

36. Ibid., p. 32.

37. Telfer, pp. 133–39.

38. Richard Hooker, *The Laws of Ecclesiastical Polity*, Book VI, chap. 15.

39. Ross, pp. 15–17; McNeill, pp. 219–40.

40. McNeill, pp. 240-45.

41. Quoted by John Stott in *Confess Your Sins* (Philadelphia: The Westminster Press, 1964), p. 87.

42. Quoted by Stott, p. 89. Emphasis added.

43. Gunstone, p. 75.

Chapter III. Contemporary Rites of Reconciliation

1. Max Thurian, *Confession*, trans. Edwin Hudson (London: SCM, 1958) and Stephan Richter, *Metanoia: Christian Penance and Confession*, trans. Raymond Kelly (New York: Sheed and Ward, 1966).

2. Harry McSorley, "Luther and Trent on the Faith Needed for the Sacrament of Penance," in *Sacramental Reconciliation*, vol. 61 *Concilium: Religion in the Seventies*, ed. Edward Schillebeeckx (New York: Herder and Herder, 1971).

3. This development is helpfully sketched in Hatchett, *Commentary* (see chap. 2, n. 33), pp. 11–12.

4. Monika Hellwig, *Sign of Reconciliation and Conversion* (Wilmington, Del.: M. Glazier, 1983), p. 89.

5. *The Book of Common Prayer* (New York: The Church Hymnal Corporation, 1979). Page numbers from the *BCP* are included in the text.

6. In the Celebration and Blessing of a marriage, we pray for the couple: "Give them grace, when they hurt each other, to recognize their fault, and to seek each other's forgiveness and yours." (p. 429); and in the Burial Office, Rite 1, there is the petition: "Grant to thy faithful people pardon and peace, that we may be cleansed from all sin and serve thee with a quiet mind." (p. 481).

7. I have taken this distinction from a 1659 work by the Anglican apologist Harmon L'Estrange in *The Alliance of Divine Office*, quoted by McNeill in his *History of the Cure of Souls* (see chap. 2, n. 16), p. 233.

8. Hatchett, p. 423.

9. For a more extended analysis of the rubrics, see ibid., pp. 453–54.

10. Cf. Loren Gavitt, ed., *St. Augustine's Prayer Book*, rev. ed. (West Park, N.Y.: Holy Cross Publications, 1967), pp. 122–24 and E. H. Maddux, ed., *A Manual for Priests of the American Church*, 5th ed. (Cambridge, Mass.: Society of St. John the Evangelist, 1970), pp. 21–24.

11. Hatchett, pp. 455–56. It should be noted that this form is not the one eventually adopted in the *Ordo Paenitentiae* of 1974, of which more below.

12. For a complete listing of the sources, see ibid., pp. 456–58.

13. *The Rite of Penance*, trans. International Commission on English in the Liturgy (New York: Catholic Book Publishing Co., 1975).

14. J. D. Crichton, *The Ministry of Reconciliation* (London: Geoffrey Chapman, 1974), pp. 11–12.

15. Ralph Keifer and Frederick R. McManus, *The Rite of Penance Commentaries, Vol. I: Understanding the Document* (Washington, D.C.: The Liturgical Conference, 1975), p. vi.

16. Godfrey Diekmann, "The New Rite of Penance: A Theological Evaluation," in *The Rite of Penance Commentaries, Vol III: Background and Directions*, ed. Nathan Mitchell (Washington, D.C.: The Liturgical Conference, 1978), p. 82.

17. Preface to Keifer and McManus, p. iii. The Jesuit theologian, Ladislas Orsy in *The Evolving Church and the Sacrament of Penance* (Denville, N.J.: Dimension Books, 1978), pp. 132–60, takes a dissenting view and claims that the rite broke no new theological ground but only reiterated the Tridentine view of the matter.

18. *Rite*, p. 11.

19. Ibid., p. 13

20. Ibid., pp. 14–15.

21. Ibid., pp. 16–18.

22. Ibid., pp. 24–25.

23. Ibid., pp. 19–20 (Introduction), and pp. 43–71 (text of the rite). The text of the absolution is:

> God, the Father of mercies, through the death and resurrection of his son has reconciled the world to himself and sent the Holy Spirit among us for the forgiveness of sins; through the ministry of the Church may God give you pardon and peace, and I absolve you from your sins in the name of the Father, and of the Son, + and of the Holy Spirit.

24. Keifer and McManus, p. 3.

25. Colman Grabert, "The Rite of Penance/Reconciliation: Christian Existence in a Reconciled Humanity," in Mitchell, *Background and Directions* (see above, n. 16), p. 107.

26. Ibid., p. 117.

27. Ibid., p. 108.

28. Keifer and Mcmanus, p. 43.

29. Karl Rahner, *The Church and the Sacraments*, trans. W. T. O'Hara (New York: Herder and Herder, 1963), pp. 14–15.

30. Keifer and McManus, pp. 19, 23.

31. Crichton, p. 29.

32. Keifer and McManus, p. 29.

33. Tad Guzie and John McIlhon, *the Forgiveness of Sin* (Chicago: Thomas More Press, 1979), pp. 102–5.

34. Crichton, p. 24.

35. Richter, *Metanoia* (see above, n. 1), p. 97.

36. Dietrich Bonhoeffer, *Life Together*, trans. John Doberstein (New York: Harper and Brothers, 1954), pp. 110, 112.

37. Herbert Girgensohn, *Baptism—Confession—The Lord's Supper, vol. 2 of Teaching Luther's Cathechism*, trans. John W. Doberstein (Philadelphia: Muhlenberg Press, 1960).

38. Ibid., p. 67.

39. Ibid., pp. 75–86.

40. Ibid., p. 82.

41. Walter Bouman, "Confession-Absolution and the Eucharisitc Liturgy," *The Lutheran Quarterly* 26 (May 1974), p. 218.

42. *The Lutheran Book of Worship*, Minister's Desk Ed. (Minneapolis: Augsburg Publishing House, 1978), pp. 322–23.

43. Ibid., pp. 34–35.

44. Philip Pfatteicher and Carlos Messerlie, *Manual on the Liturgy: The Lutheran Book of Worship* (Minneapolis: Augsburg Publishing House, 1979), pp. 192–95.

45. Timothy Ware, *The Orthodox Church* (New York: Penguin Books, 1963), pp. 245–47, and Franz Nikolasch, "The Sacrament of Penance: Learning from the East," trans. Mark Hollebone in Schillebeeckx, *Sacramental Reconciliation*, pp. 65–76.

46. Max Thurian, *Confession*, trans. Edward Hudson (London: SCM, 1958).

47. Ibid., pp. 52–53.

48. Ibid., p. 54.

49. Ibid., p. 139.

50. George W. Bowman, *The Dynamics of Confession* (Richmond, Va.: John Knox Press, 1969).

51. Ibid., p. 54.

52. Thomas C. Oden, *Pastoral Theology: Essentials of Ministry* (San Francisco: Harper and Row, 1983), p. 175.

53. Richard J. Foster, *Celebration of Discipline* (San Francisco: Harper and Row, 1978), pp. 127–29.

54. Ibid., p. 137.

55. Orsy, p. 30.

56. Ross, p. 9.

57. Urban T. Holmes III, *Turning to Christ: A Theology of Renewal and Evangelization* (New York: Seabury Press, 1981), p. 101. The whole fifth chapter of this book elaborates a far more profound understanding of conversion than we can here.

58. Nathan Mitchell, "Conversion and Reconciliation in the New Testament: The Parable of the Cross," in Mitchell, *Background and Directions*, p. 13.

59. Holmes, *Turning to Christ*, pp. 93ff.

60. Léonce Hamelin, *Reconciliation in the Church*, trans. Matthew O'Connell (Collegeville, Minn.: Liturgical Press, 1980), p. 53.

61. Hellwig, p. 107.

62. Mitchell, "Conversion and Reconciliation," p. 8. Emphasis in the original.

63. Hellwig, p. 26.

64. Guzie and McIlhon, p. 111.
65. Mitchell, "Conversion and Reconciliation," p. 16. Emphasis in the original.
66. Gunstone, p. 83.
67. See, for example, *Baptism, Eucharist and Ministry: Faith and Order Paper No. 111* (Geneva: World Council of Churches, 1982), or, within the Episcopal Church, A. Theodore Eastman, *The Baptizing Community* (New York: Seabury Press, 1982).
68. Godfrey Diekmann, "Reconciliation Through the Prayer of the Community," in Mitchell, *Background and Directions*, p. 49.
69. Hellwig, p. 93.
70. Crichton, p. 30.
71. Hellwig, pp. 145–46.
72. Hamelin, p. 73.
73. Mitchell, "Conversion and Reconciliation," p. 63.
74. Ibid., p. 16.
75. Guzie and McIlhon, p. 111.
76. Robert Farrar Capon, *Hunting the Divine Fox: Images and Mystery in Christian Faith* (New York: Seabury Press, 1974), p. 151.

Chapter IV. Pastoral Resources for Reconciliation

1. Primary references are: Tilden Edwards, *Spiritual Friend* (New York/Ramsey, N.J.: Paulist Press, 1980), Urban T. Holmes III, *A History of Christian Spirituality: An Analytical Introduction* (New York: Seabury Press, 1980), Kenneth Leech, *Soul Friend* (London: Sheldon Press, 1977), and Martin Thornton, *English Spirituality: An Outline of Ascetical Theology According to the English Pastoral Tradition* (London: SPCK, 1963). These are representative and not exhaustive; their bibliographies contain abundant further references.
2. Thornton, pp. 48–52.
3. Ibid., p. 16.
4. Ibid., p. 26.
5. Leech, p. 38.
6. Thornton, p. 290.
7. Edwards, p. 125.
8. Karl Rahner, *Theological Investigations*, vol. 3 *The Theology of the Spiritual Life*, trans. Karl-H. Kreuger and Boniface Kreuger (Baltimore: Helicon Press, 1967, p. 10.
9. This development, with others, is traced in Holmes, *History*.
10. Rahner, *Theology of the Spiritual Life*, p. 13.
11. Leech, p. 37.

12. Rahner, *Theology of the Spiritual Life*, p. 16.

13. Leech, p. 59.

14. Thornton, p. 36.

15. Gunstone, *The Liturgy of Penance* (see chap. 2, n. 2), p. 49.

16. Edwards, p. 94.

17. Leech, p. 195.

18. Ibid., p. 208.

19. Thornton, p. 300.

20. Holmes, *History*, p. 161.

21. Paul Mussen and Nancy Eisenberg-Berg, *Roots of Caring, Sharing and Helping: The Development of Pro-Social Behavior* (San Francisco: W. H. Freeman and Company, 1977).

22. Mussen and Eisenberg-Berg, pp. 2–4.

23. Ibid., pp. 25–28, and Robert B. Ewen *An Introduction to Theories of Personality* (New York: Academic Press, 1980), pp. 18–30.

24. Ewen, pp. 71–112, and Calvin S. Hall and Vernon J. Nordby, *A Primer of Jungian Psychology* (New York: New American Library, 1973), pp. 81–95.

25. See, for example, Daniel J. Levinson et al., *The Seasons in a Man's Life* (New York: Ballantine Books, 1978) for an elaboration of adult development in males, and Evelyn Eaton Whitehead and James D. Whitehead, *Christian Life Patterns: The Psychological Challenges and Religious Invitations of Adult Life* (Garden City, N.Y.: Doubleday and Company, 1979) for an explicitly Christian reflection on Eriksonian theory.

26. Robert G. Kegan, "There the Dance Is: Religious Dimensions of Developmental Framework," in Christiane Brusselmans et al., *Toward Moral and Religious Maturity*, First International Conference on Moral and Religious Development (Glenview, Ill.: Silver Burdett Company, 1980), p. 406. Emphasis in the original.

27. This theory is delightfully laid out in a fictitious dialogue with Erik Erikson and Lawrence Kohlberg, whose work we will encounter below, in James W. Fowler, *Stages of Faith: The Psychology of Human Development and the Quest for Meaning* (San Francisco: Harper and Row, 1981), pp. 37–85.

28. Ronald Goldman, *Religious Thinking from Childhood to Adolescence*, American ed. (New York: The Seabury Press, 1968) and *Readiness for Religion: A Basis for Developmental Religious Education*, American ed. (New York: The Seabury Press, 1969).

29. Mussen and Eisenberg-Berg, pp. 110–15.

30. Quoted in ibid., p. 116.

31. Quoted in Anne Colby et al., *A Longitudinal Sudy of Moral Judgment*, Monographs of the Society for Research in Child Development, serial no. 200, vol. 48, nos. 1–2 (n.p., 1983), p. 1. This monograph sum-

marizes twenty years of research, including validation, further developments and efforts at empirical verification, some of it done cross-culturally.

32. Mussen and Eisenberg-Berg, p. 120.

33. William Rogers, "Interdisciplinary Approaches to Moral and Religious Development: A Critical Overview," in Brusselmans et al., p. 22. Emphasis in original. This article provides a fine survey of the whole range of research and theory about moral and religious development, with cogent models for correlating them.

34. Enda McDonagh, "Moral Theology and Moral Development," in Brusselmans et al., pp. 334–35.

35. Carol Gilligan, *In a Different Voice: Psychological Theory and Women's Development* (Cambridge, Mass.: Harvard University Press, 1982).

36. Ibid., p. 17.

37. Ibid., p. 19.

38. Ibid., p. 69.

39. Ibid., p. 105.

40. Ibid., p. 71.

41. Ibid., p. 174.

42. Mussen and Eisenberg-Berg, pp. 28–39.

43. Ibid., p. 126.

44. Ibid., pp. 123–30.

45. Ibid., p. 159.

46. F. Clark Power and Lawrence Kohlberg, "Religion, Morality and Ego Development," in Brusselmans et al., p. 351.

47. Ibid., pp. 351–52.

48. Ibid., p. 369.

49. Ibid., p. 367.

50. Enda McDonagh, "Moral Theology and Moral Development," in Brusselmans et al., p. 341.

51. Our description of the "stages of faith" comes from Fowler's principal work by that name, cited previously, and a shorter summary in James W. Fowler, "Faith and the Structuring of Meaning," in Brusselmans et al., pp. 51–85.

52. Fowler, "Faith and the Structuring of Meaning," pp. 64–65.

53. This analysis comes from Power and Kohlberg, p. 353.

54. These are elaborated and schematized in Fowler, "Faith and the Structuring of Meaning," pp. 74–79.

55. Fowler, "Faith and the Structuring of Meaning," p. 84.

56. Rogers, "Interdisciplinary Approaches," p. 37.

57. James A. O'Donohoe, "Moral and Faith Developmental Theory" in Brusselmans et al., pp. 393–98.

58. Fritz Oser, "Stages of Religious Judgment" in Brusselmans et al., pp. 277–315.

59. John H. Westerhoff III, *Will Our Children Have Faith?* (New York: The Seabury Press, 1976), p. 89.

60. These are developed in *Will Our Children Have Faith?* (New York: The Seaury Press, 1976), pp. 89–99.

61. Holmes, *Turning to Christ* (see chap. 3, n. 57), pp. 162–68.

62. Ibid., pp. 169–177.

63. Robert G. Kegan, "There the Dance Is: Religious Dimensions of a Developmental Framework," in Brusselmans et al., p. 407.

64. Ibid., p. 437.

65. This complex and challenging view is elaborated in Stanley Hauerwas, "Character, Narrative, and Growth in the Christian Life," in Brusselmans et al., pp. 441–84, and in his other works, which are cited in the article.

66. Hauerwas, p. 445.

67. Westerhoff, *Will Our Children Have Faith?*, p. 98.

68. Gilligan, *In a Different Voice*, pp. 106–27.

69. Gilligan, "Justice and Responsibility: Thinking about Real Dilemmas of Moral Conflict and Choice," in Brusselmans et al., p. 238.

70. McDonagh, p. 340. Emphasis in original.

71. Kegan, p. 426. Emphasis in original.

72. Holmes, *Turning to Christ*, p. 179.

73. For a more complete discussion of individuation and especially Jung's understanding of the role of religion in it, see Mary Ann Mattoon, *Jungian Psychology in Perspective* (New York: The Free Press, 1981), pp. 163–205.

Chapter V. Reconciliation in Pastoral Practice

1. In the section of *St. Augustine's Prayer Book* (see chap. 3, n. 10) entitled "The Christian's Obligations," annual confession at Easter and when needed for mortal sin is listed as one of the "Six Precepts of the Church: Being the Irreducible Minimum of Catholic Practice."

2. Holmes, *Turning to Christ* (see chap. 3, n. 57), p. xi.

3. Quoted in Hatchett, *Commentary* (see chap. 2, n. 33), pp. 450–51.

4. *Journal of the General Convention*, 1976, C-1.

5. Don Browning, *The Moral Context of Pastoral Care* (Philadelphia: Westminster Press, 1976), p. 20.

6. Ibid., pp. 21–50.

7. Clebsch and Jaekle, *Pastoral Care in Historical Perspective*, quoted

in Browning, pp. 57–59. An analysis similar to Browning's is made by Thomas Oden in the first chapter of his *Pastoral Theology* (see chap. 3, n. 52), pp. 3–15. McNeill has traced the *History of The Cure of Souls* largely in terms of Reconciliation and its evolution.

   8. Browning, p. 93. Emphasis in original.

   9. Ibid., p. 95.

   10. Ibid., p. 100.

   11. Westerhoff, *Will Our Children Have Faith?* (see chap. 4, n. 59), p. 78.

   12. James O'Donohoe, "Moral and Faith Development Theory," in Brusselmans et al (see chap. 4, n. 26), pp. 381–85.

   13. Guzie and McIlhon, *Forgiveness* (see chap. 3, n. 33), p. 152.

   14. Browning, p. 102.

   15. Hamelin, *Reconciliation in the Church* (see chap. 3, n. 60), p. 71. Emphasis in original.

   16. Ibid., p. 68.

   17. Leech, *Soul Friend* (see chap. 4, n. 1), p. 209.

   18. Hellwig, *Sign of Reconciliation and Conversion* (see chap. 3, n. 4), pp. 136–41.

   19. Crichton: *The Ministry of Reconciliation* (see chap. 3, n. 14), p. 33.

   20. Guzie and McIlhon, pp. 129, 135.

   21. Thurian, *Confession* (see chap. 3, n. 1), p. 101.

   22. Hamelin, p. 92.

   23. Ross, *Hearing Confessions* (see chap. 2, n. 6), pp. 26–29.

   24. Thurian, p. 108.

   25. Raymond Studzinski, "The Minister of Reconciliation: Some Historical Models," in Nathan Mitchell, ed., *Background and Directions* (see chap. 3, n. 16), pp. 53, 55.

   26. Ibid., pp. 56–58.

   27. Leech, pp. 213–15.

   28. Studzinski pp. 58–59.

   29. Hellwig, p. 136.

   30. Leech, pp. 212–13.

   31. Ross, p. 22.

   32. Francis G. Belton, *A Manual for Confessors*, rev. ed. (London: A. R. Mowbray, 1931), pp. 121–41.

   33. Ross, pp. 36–37.

   34. Ibid., pp. 43–47, for example.

   35. Leech, p. 216.

   36. Bonhoeffer, *Life Together* (see chap. 3, n. 36), p. 120.

   37. Belton, pp. 90–94; Leech, pp. 216–17; Ross, pp. 69–72; Thurian, pp. 111–14.

38. Leech, p. 216. Emphasis in original.

39. Ibid., p. 213.

40. Guzie and McIlhon, pp. 25–62.

41. Hauerwas, "Character, Growth and Narrative in the Christian Life," in Brusselmans et al., p. 465.

42. Leech, pp. 218–23.

43. Guzie and McIlhon, pp. 78–94.

44. *St. Augustine's Prayer Book*, pp. 112–13.

45. Ibid., pp. 113–21.

46. *How to Make a Confession* (West Park, N.Y.: Holy Cross Publications, n.d.), p. 2.

47. Ibid., p. 3.

48. Ibid., pp. 5–14.

49. Dag Hammarskjöld, *Markings*, trans. Leif Sjöberg and W. H. Auden (London: Faber and Faber, 1964), p. 87. This work is especially interesting, as Fowler believes that Hammarskjöld probably attained Stage 6. This collection of diary-like observations of life traces his pilgrimage.

50. A good place to begin this exploration is A. Theodore Eastman's fine book, *The Baptizing Community* (New York: The Seabury Press, 1982), with its helpful suggestions for baptismal instruction and practice in a corporate context.

51. See, for example, Elizabeth McMahon Jeep, ed., *The Rite of Penance Commentaries, Vol. II: Implementing the Rite* (Washington, D.C.: The Liturgical Conference, 1967), which includes a valuable list of progrms and resources.

52. Leech, p. 49.

53. Ross, pp. 79–80.

54. Ibid., p. 108.

55. Guzie and McIlhon, p. 136.

56. Charles Curran, "Examination of Conscience," in Jeep, *Implementing the Rite*, p. 36.

57. Ross, p. 56.

58. Dennis G. Michno, *A Priest's Handbook* (Wilton, Conn.: Morehouse-Barlow, 1983), p. 232.

59. Ross, pp. 60–62.

60. Quoted by Leech, p. 215.

61. Guzie and McIlhon, p. 133.

62. Thurian, p. 114.

Select Bibliography

Belton, Francis G. *A Manual for Confessors*. London: A. R. Mowbray, 1931.

Bonhoeffer, Dietrich. *Life Together*. Translated by John W. Doberstein. New York: Harper and Brothers, 1954.

The Book of Common Prayer. New York: The Church Hymnal Corp., 1976.

Bouman, Walter R. "Confession, Absolution and the Eucharistic Liturgy," *The Lutheran Quarterly* 26 (May 1974): 204–20.

Bowman, George W. *The Dynamics of Confession*. Richmond, Va.: John Knox Press, 1969.

Browning, Don S. *The Moral Context of Pastoral Care*. Philadelphia: Westminster Press, 1976.

Brusselmans, Christine, et al. *Toward Moral and Religious Maturity*. The First International Conference on Moral and Religious Development. Morristown, N.J.: Silver Burdett Co., 1980.

Crichton, J. C. *The Ministry of Reconciliation*. London: Geoffrey Chapman, 1974.

Edwards, Tilden. *Spiritual Friend*. New York/Ramsey, N.J.: Paulist Press, 1980.

Erikson, Erik H. *Identity, Youth and Crisis*. New York: W. W. Norton, 1968.

Ewen, Robert B. *An Introduction to Theories of Personality*. New York: Academic Press, 1980.

Foster, Richard J. *Celebration of Discipline*. San Francisco: Harper and Row, 1978.

Fowler, James W. *Stages of Faith*. San Francisco: Harper and Row, 1981.

Gavitt, Loren, ed. *St. Augustine's Prayer Book*. rev. ed. West Park, N.Y.: Holy Cross Publications, 1967.

Gilligan, Carol. *In a Different Voice: Psychological Theory and Women's Development*. Cambridge, Mass.: Harvard University Press, 1982.

Girgensohn, Herbert. *Baptism—Confession—The Lord's Supper*. vol. 2 of

Teaching Luther's Catechism. Translated by John W. Doberstein. Philadelphia: Muhlenberg Press, 1960.

Gunstone, J. A. L. *The Liturgy of Penance*. London: Faith Press, 1966.

Guzie, Tad and McIlhon, John. *The Forgiveness of Sin*. Chicago: Thomas More Press, 1979.

Hall, Calvin S. and Nordby, Vernon J. *A Primer of Jungian Psychology*. New York: New American Library, 1973.

Hamelin, Léonce. *Reconciliation in the Church*. Translated by Matthew O'Connell. Collegeville, Minn.: Liturgical Press, 1980.

Hatchett, Marion J. *Commentary on the American Prayer Book*. New York: The Seabury Press, 1980.

Hellwig, Monika. *Sign of Reconciliation and Conversion*. Wilmington, Del.: M. Glazier, 1982.

Holmes, Urban T., III. *A History of Christian Spirituality: An Analytical Introduction*. New York: The Seabury Press, 1980.

————. *Turning to Christ: A Theology of Renewal and Evangelization*. New York: The Seabury Press, 1981.

How to Make a Confession. West Park, N.Y.: Holy Cross Publications, n.d.

Jeep, Elizabeth McMahon, ed. *Implementing the Rite*. The Rite of Penance Commentaries, vol. 2. Washington, D.C.: The Liturgical Conference, 1976.

Keifer, Ralph and McManus, Frederick R. *Understanding the Document*. The Rite of Penance Commentaries, vol. 3. Washington, D.C.: The Liturgical Conference, 1975.

Leech, Kenneth. *Soul Friend*. London: Sheldon Press, 1977.

Lutheran Book of Worship. Minister's Desk Edition. Minneapolis: Augsburg Publishing House, 1978.

Maddux, E. H. *A Manual for Priests of the American Church*. 5th ed. Cambridge, Mass.: Society of St. John the Evangelist, 1970.

McNeill, John T. *A History of the Cure of Souls*. New York: Harper and Row, 1951.

Michno, Dennis G. *A Priest's Handbook*. Wilton, Conn.: Morehouse-Barlow, 1983.

Mitchell, Nathan, ed. *Background and Directions*. The Rite of Penance Commentaries, vol. 3. Washington, D.C.: The Liturgical Conference, 1978.

Mortimer, Robert Cecil. *The Origins of Private Penance in the Western Church*. Oxford: The Clarendon Press, 1939.

Mussen, Paul and Eisenberg-Berg, Nancy. *Roots of Caring, Sharing, and Helping: The Development of Pro-Social Behavior in Children*. San Francisco: W. H. Freeman and Co., 1977.

Oakley, Thomas Pollock. *English Penitential Discipline and Anglo-Saxon Law in Their Joint Influence*. Columbia University Studies in the Social Sciences, no. 242, 1923. Reprint. New York: A.M.S. Press, 1969.

Oden, Thomas C. *Pastoral Theology*. San Francisco: Harper and Row, 1983.

Orsy, Ladislas. *The Evolving Church and the Sacrament of Penance*. Denville, N.J.: Dimension Books, 1978.

Pfatteicher, Philip H. and Messerli, Carlos R. *Manual on the Liturgy: Lutheran Book of Worship*. Minneapolis: Augsburg Publishing House, 1979.

Poschmann, B. *Penance and the Anointing of the Sick*. New York: Herder and Herder, 1964.

Rahner, Karl. *Theological Investigation*. Vol. 3: *The Theology of the Spiritual Life*. Translated by Kark-H. Kruger and Boniface Kruger. Baltimore: Helicon Press, 1967.

———. *Theological Investigations*. Vol. 15: *Penance in the Early Church*. Translated by Lionel Swain. New York: Crossroads, 1982.

Richter, Stephan. *Metanoia: Christian Penance and Confession*. Translated by Raymond Kelly. New York: Sheed and Ward, 1966.

Rituale Romanum. *The Rite of Penance*. English translation by the International Commission on English in the Liturgy. New York: Catholic Book Publishing Co., 1975.

Ross, Kenneth. *Hearing Confessions*. London: S. P. C. K., 1974.

Schillebeeckx, Edward, ed. *Sacramental Reconciliation*. Concilium, vol 61. New York: Herder and Herder, 1971.

Stott, John R. *Confess Your Sins: The Way of Reconciliation*. American ed. Philadelphia: Westminster Press, 1965.

Telfer, William. *The Forgiveness of Sins*. Philadelphia: Muhlenberg Press, 1960.

Tentler, Thomas N. *Sin and Confession on the Eve of the Reformation*. Princeton, N.J.: Princeton University Press, 1977.

Thornton, Martin. *English Spirituality: An Outline of Ascetical Theology According to the English Pastoral Tradition*. London: S. P. C. K., 1963.

Thurian, Max. *Confession*. Translated by Edwin Hudson. London: S. C. M., 1958.

Ware, Timothy. *The Orthodox Church*. New York: Penguin Books, 1963.

Westerhoff, John H., III. *Will Our Children Have Faith?* New York: The Seabury Press, 1976.

Whitehead, Evelyn Eaton and Whitehead, James D. *Christian Life Patterns: The Psychological Challenges and Religious Invitations of Adult Life*. Garden City, N.Y.: Doubleday and Co., 1979.